Rona Frye hails from Lake Geneva, Wisconsin, in the heart of the Midwest and a very thriving small town. She grew up living in the woods, rivers, and nature, which created a deep love and comfort in the outdoors. Being free equaled happiness, while married life, doing what everyone else was doing, felt lonely like 'Groundhog Day.' When she could walk out the door as a kid and not come back until she was hungry, that feeling of freedom and immersion in nature and exploration fed her spirit, As she peeled away the layers of the life she was leading after her kids were raised and her marriage was dead, she decided to change everything up, toss to the curb all that did not serve her highest good, and go on the road. She took off for parts unknown to discover herself and her world. There was no plan, just a calling to open up to whatever showed up. This nomadic journey took fourteen years of twists and turns, joy, and pain but most of all the realization that she was unafraid to face the unknown, uncertainty, and go solo. Her childhood taught her to be resilient and to depend on herself alone for strength and guidance.

She birthed a highly successful interior decorating business, raised three beautiful children, earned a top-secret clearance from the U.S. government through military intelligence work, drove through all of Mexico all the way down Central America to a caretaking gig in the jungle, faced every uncomfortable moment with curiosity and the knowing that she would always come out on top, and authored books about what she learned through studying people, places, and lifestyles.

This book is dedicated to Julia, John, and Jennifer. They were along for the magic carpet ride. And they are my greatest teachers.

Rona Frye

TOSSED INTO THE DEEP END

AUSTIN MACAULEY PUBLISHERS™

LONDON • CAMBRIDGE • NEW YORK • SHARJAH

Ordering Information
Quantity sales: Special discounts are available on quantity purchases by corporations, associations, and others. For details, contact the publisher at the address below.

Publisher's Cataloging-in-Publication data
Frye, Rona
Tossed into the Deep End

ISBN 9781647500023 (Paperback)
ISBN 9781645367116 (Hardback)
ISBN 9781647500030 (ePub e-book)

Library of Congress Control Number: 2020915521

www.austinmacauley.com/us

First Published (2020)
Austin Macauley Publishers LLC
40 Wall Street, 28th Floor
New York, NY 10005
USA

mail-usa@austinmacauley.com
+1 (646) 5125767

Table of Contents

Hoop Jumping Expert

Also known as codependent extraordinaire, I wore that badge for the first 70 years of my life before I cracked the code. Many books, seminars, girlfriend discussions, therapy, and just plain soul-seeking led me to the discovery that I could kick that behavior to the curb and start loving myself first. Putting me first felt wrong on every level for a very long time until it slowly began to actually feel good.

The first step, almost like the 12-step thing for addictions, which this actually is, was when an old school friend stopped by to visit me. I was neck deep into building an interior decorating business, helping my 13-year-old wade through the throngs of puberty, mining the wreckage of my marriage, stepping through the minefields of menopause and low and behold; she noted that I forgot how to laugh!!!

I used to laugh easily. Codependency had me by the balls. I didn't see it, didn't know it was even there but it was the elephant in the room.

This friend of mine from school used to be a real party girl, wild and crazy while I was pretty tame by comparison. The new Gibby was 'born again,' married for the third time, and on a brand-new path. Her goal was to 'fix' people. I was very familiar with that idea myself. A big part of codependency had to do with fixing people. Anyone who earns the title of 'fixer' or 'helper' knows that everyone else comes first, everyone in the room 'must' be happy or else, and it is her job to see that they are, which means that the 'helpers' needs come in dead last.

Altha was a codependent master as well as playing a double role as victim/martyr. That is no easy path in life, but she was entrenched in that role.

I knew when I was in my mid-teens that it was up to me to protect her. She wasn't doing it, so it had to fall on me. Someone had to do it! I couldn't stand to watch her, fight after fight, year after year, fall into a heap of tears when Homer picked on her in his drunken stupor. If she put the salt and pepper shaker on the table wrong, it was food for a fight.

Looking back, the scene was well-laid out, a perfect setup for me to step right into that job. I took it seriously too. I felt some kind of weird power taking this situation on.

In the middle of dysfunction, everyone was so busy with their own twisted role that they didn't see the forest. We were all trees banging into each other. If we got our act together and figured it out, we could have been a forest. But we were bobbleheads bumping into each other, never seeing the game we were all playing.

At the head of the ridiculous frenzy was Homer; the drunk, pervert, sociopath, husband. His copilot, Altha, was the martyr, victim, child bride, disillusioned, hidden agenda, secretive, angry, resentful, ever-annoyed, two-sided, wife. Then, they went ahead and had eight kids.

Talk about the perfect storm; along came a series of train wrecks. It was like they were operating blindly using the Braille system.

"Oops, we're having another baby. Oh, god, what about you, wait, you're one and a half-years-old, it is freaking time for you to grow the hell up, another baby is about to show up and we cannot be having two in diapers. Oh no! That's not happening. So, you need to get your shit together and get trained up and out of those diapers now. And don't be getting all stubborn about it either. That'll just piss me off." Yep, that kind of sums up their method of operation.

They were pushed to the brink with one child and then went ahead and had seven more. Then, they were really mad. Altha now hates sex because it is the source of the problem. She made sure that all of her kids were on the same page by shaming them anytime they showed any interest in dating. They lay their burdens on us kids because, why not? This couldn't have been their faults. Instead, they made sure everyone was fully aware of their misery. That way we had no choice. And we each had to figure out what our individual roles were in making things better. We became fixers.

After I stepped up to the plate and pushed Homer back a couple times to cut down on his verbal abuse of Altha, I went ahead and got married too. And just so you know, I picked someone with every single issue I was familiar with. I hooked up with a guy who gave it all back to me.

Though I was unhappy from day one, I stayed anyway because that's what I saw Altha and Homer do. Their role modeling showed us all that you just stayed the hell in the middle of all of your shit storms because that is 'what we do.' Nobody fixes anything, no one gets counseling, and no one knew ways of resolving things. Just keep motoring through. No wonder to this day I hate the idea of Groundhog Day, anything repetitive.

My marriage lasted 28 years. I was already lonely at the wedding reception. The honeymoon was all about him fishing and then it was all about him hanging out with his friends. I used to wonder; *didn't people get married so they could spend time together?*

But you know I just jumped through more hoops, thinking, maybe I'm not fun enough, maybe I'm not smart enough, or maybe I'm not interesting enough. Whatever was off-kilter, I assumed it was me that was the kink in the works. I had to fix me. So, I wandered around feeling like shit, thinking I had to find a way to be a better wife. Maybe I could clean the house better, I could always be ready and available for sex, I could cook better, and garden better.

I had Altha and Homer rolled into one right here in my life. He was packaged up perfectly with all that familiar baggage. I was beginning to see the picture clearer. And I was so filled with longing and hunger and desire for more fulfillment. I was so lonely. I would have been thrilled if he just looked at me, sat with me, ate with me, and walked with me.

At one point I wondered if he and Altha got some kind of power from denying the love and attention that I begged for from them. I came to believe they did. One day I tried out my theory with my mother. I stopped begging from her. I let her ignore me, discount me, make me feel less, ignore me some more, listen to everyone else but me, praise everyone else but me, and I stopped caring. She saw it. I could see a difference in her reaction to me. She never let me in on what she was feeling or seeing, but I could tell that she knew something changed. But the change was real and for keeps now. No more hoop jumping to win her over.

As far as Fritz, enough went down during those 28 years that I woke up to the predicament I was in with him, knew I needed more, and realized it was up to me to get it. I had to find a way to save myself. I had these epiphanies one after another. The monumental one was when he decided that we both should wing it rather than protect ourselves during sex to prevent pregnancy. I knew it was time to go off of birth control and asked that he get the vasectomy, or I could get my tubes tied. He wanted neither. He said he would handle it by 'pulling out' in time. I handed over so much of my power to him that day and it would bring so much anguish to me that it was the beginning of the end.

I got pregnant within two months and since he had already made it clear he didn't want more children, abortion was the only answer. This is where I cringe at how much I handed over my power and life to him. He had my life and a future soul's life in his hands. I went through the motions to line up an abortion and knew it had to happen in the first trimester. 'We' went to see the doctor for that treatment. I could see and feel that the doctor did not want to be doing this work. But he did. When he was done with what was called a 'vacuum aspiration,' he said that I could come back for a post-op exam. In my mind I had this sense that I must do that. On the day of the post-op the doc examined me and ruled me 'good to go.' I left there feeling exactly like I did the time before and exactly like I did before the treatment. Something didn't seem right.

I returned to work and my belly continued to grow and then one day I felt a kick. I was now wearing big shirts to hide my growing belly because I worked in a basement custom drapery store where six women and I handmade window treatments and all sorts of custom décor for our customers. In that basement work environment, I had already witnessed one of the women share something very sensitive with the others and another of those women crushingly using it against her. It was not a safe environment for me to be sharing my story. I had to hide it and figure it out by myself.

I went to my GP for an exam and consultation to figure out what was going on. He was appalled because his response to me was,

"Well, of course you're pregnant."

He was the doctor who gave me the name of the abortion doctor. I reminded him that I had the abortion, so how could this be? He shrugged his shoulders dismissively and said, "Better call that doctor."

I did and that doctor lined up a more extreme abortion process in a bigger hospital. Now I was headed for a more difficult situation and all because I allowed Fritz to direct the course of my life. I was the only one suffering. This might sound mean and thoughtless, but he was just like Altha, detached. He was physically present but emotionally absent. He and Altha were able to give zero love and nurturing; it was a skill they had. I found it puzzling because I felt too much. They seemed to feel nothing.

I went through the more difficult process with Fritz, sitting in a chair beside my bed reading the newspaper. The process was said to be quick and I would be out that day,

14

within hours. A saline solution would be introduced into my womb and that would speed up the process. By now, even if I wanted to keep this baby, I had to wonder what was sucked out by that doc? Did I have two babies and he took one or what? This is the part that is tormenting to think about. Feeling life inside me, it was only natural to want this baby. But I'd already dug a hole so deep that I didn't believe I could change my mind now.

It turned out that things didn't go like normal for me. Hours went by with me still lingering. Finally, the nurse stepped in, pulled back my blankets and sheets and found that I had hemorrhaged all over the bed. She decided right then to expedite things and got another nurse to come in. Together they induced labor and made things happen. I was put in a wheelchair for a D&C next and then released.

Unfortunately, I was now quite weak and standing, walking or being in the elevator made me want to black out. The toll on me was more than I realized. And if that wasn't all sad enough, we went back to our house where Altha was babysitting the kids and I sat down to tell her what I'd just been through. I sat there sobbing my heart out and I saw her sitting in a chair across from me looking at me like, 'huh, yeah, and so?' She saw me crushed and broken by this experience and she was able to look at me with zero compassion, love or tenderness. That was so jarring and sad that it helped me see what I had in these two people who were the two pillars I needed to lean on but these two were not pillars, they were empty shells.

I went back to work the next day and buried all of it. It never went away; I just threw a rug over it. But there was something undeniable inside my soul that was dying from this life and yet trying to cling to it. Like being smothered and gasping desperately for air. By learning to never deal, confront or resolve, I moved through life as if nothing happened. But on the inside things were changing.

That summer we had plans to spend our vacation in Hayward, Wisconsin with Fritz's best friend Jake and his wife and three kids. We also had three kids at that time, so we all motored up there, seven hours for us, to our cabins near the water. As it is always true for everyone, wherever you go, there you are. We were in a new location, but everyone was still themselves. Fiona, Jake's wife, came with her typical behavior. She stayed up late to avoid sleeping with Jake. Jake got drunk because his life sucked; Fritz and Jake got drunk or fished, or got drunk 'and' fished all day for the first two days while Fiona slept in and got up late in the morning. I was up, feeding six kids and babysitting them all; we were near the water, they were all little. Mine were eleven, eight and three and Fiona's were similar in age, just a bit older. I was the babysitter until Fiona showed up and then I was the cook until the guys decided to wander in from the bar or the lake.

Standing at the grill I had a talk with myself. *This is your only vacation all year, it is a shit sandwich of a vacation up here, what are you going to do about it?* The answer came quickly, *you are going to leave.* I announced at dinner that I was leaving. Everyone wanted to weigh in on my decision but it was too late for that. I offered my kids a choice, stay or go. My daughters opted to go. My son stayed. I packed us up in the car and started it up. Jake and Fritz tried to foolishly stand in the road but I just drove around them and headed down the road not having any idea how we got here or how to get home.

I found a motel down the road, got us a room and pulled out the atlas and studied it. There was no GPS then. In the morning we drove seven hours back home.

We had the most beautiful, peaceful rest of the week at home all by ourselves while they all stayed up in Hayward.

That courageous act was the beginning of me taking my power back. It was minor but it was the beginning. It was me deciding to consider my own happiness. From there on, with baby steps, I began to unravel the life I had in search of the life I wanted.

I started an interior decorating business and it became incredibly successful. I dove straight into menopause, Jen, my youngest was in puberty, the marriage was shot, I was beginning to get therapy to get help with my life and started working out at the YMCA. My friend Gibby continued to come over and try to remind me how to laugh. Eventually, through considerable diligence, with many walks and talks, she helped me choke out what was long-buried inside of me. Word by word, the feelings came out. I wanted out of the marriage, I wanted Fritz to be happy but not with me. Not at my expense. Those words were in there probably since the beginning, but I couldn't bring myself to voice them. I didn't know I had a right to ask for what I needed and wanted, and to put myself first.

Giving the marriage the boot was so hard! I was kicking a perfectly good human being to the curb. But I was so unhappy with him!!! None of my needs were being met with him. My life was crushingly lonely. He had to go.

From that day forward I began a journey of soul-searching; studying, reading books, and looking for a life of meaning. I was an outlier in my birth family and I had to find my way alone. When I lost all interest in anything and didn't know what I cared about, liked, or wanted, I had to turn that around and figure it out for myself. What did I want, who was I, what did I stand for, and what did I want to do now?

Todd

All of a sudden, he could not figure out how to shift his old Ford truck; something he had done for as long as he owned that beloved treasure. Just yesterday he seemed fine. Now, sitting down to play a card game he had played hundreds of times, Hand and Foot, with our mom, everything seemed confusing. Dealing, laying out the cards, and following along no longer made sense to him. Sybil and Altha were eyeing him, trying to discern what it was they were seeing. Todd didn't act unusual otherwise. He still walked normally, still ate normally, and seemed to know who everyone was, so what was going on?

Sybil asked Altha to follow her to the kitchen where they could put their heads together and come up with an answer. There was no answer though. The only option was to take Todd in to the ER for analysis. They hopped in Sybil's Tahoe, telling Todd that they wanted the docs to have a look at him. He was always a kind, gentle, and trusting, soul so there was no balking at this sudden new plan.

The drive, about half an hour long, went smoothly, no one was saying a word. There reason to worry but without answers what could they think? The docs, NAs,

RNs, and technicians moved quickly taking a scan of his head, asking questions, checking his O_2 levels, doing eye/hand coordination and the usual blood pressure, pulse, and temp vitals. Now for the waiting game to see the results. Sybil and Altha waited in the lounge as the hours passed, filled with worry and growing so weary. Altha was no spring chicken; she was closing in on 87 years of age. That made Sybil close to 69. Both advanced in age, and that is enough to find this frightening occurrence exhausting. Finally, they decided to call me and clue me in about the situation. I was the nomadic sort, often coming and going, never staying put for long. I was here in town at the moment and maybe they forgot they could count on me. I immediately dropped everything and drove into Yuma from my casita in Wheels.

The Regional Hospital on Worth Avenue was where they were. I walked in and spotted them sitting quietly, sagging in their chairs, exhausted and so troubled.

I said, "Hi" and sat with them to hear their concerns and then walked into the cubicle Todd was in and found him sitting up on a bed with the oxygen clip on his nose. Hmmm, that was not what I expected but it definitely informed me that something was very wrong. The techs came by just then and said that they read the report and found seven tumors in his brain. That was a situation out of their range of care and they advised that the next step had to be to move him to Tucson to a hospital equipped to handle this.

The transport vehicle showed up, Todd was strapped in and loaded into the back as I stood watching. Suddenly the sight made me cry. What was happening to him? He seemed so childlike, so trusting as they tucked him inside that vehicle. They were strangers and yet he was so fine with it all. How could that be? The poor guy had no idea what was going on and yet he completely trusted those men. That broke my heart.

I told Sybil and Altha to go home to rest and that I was going to follow the transport vehicle to Tucson and stay with Todd. On the ride I called my three kids and let them know what was happening. Ninety minutes later we were there. Todd was being unloaded and rolled inside. I parked and went in, staying close. Whatever was going to happen I would be a part of. I knew, without really knowing, that he was not capable, right now, of understanding where he was, who he was, what was going on, and I did not want him scared or lost.

He was set up in a private room on the third floor and very quickly the room was filled with machines hooked up to him one way or another. I let the nurse know that I would be staying there, in the room, with Todd and would need a cot, blanket, pillow and water. My daughter, Julia, called and talked to her at that time and told her to take good care of her mom. The nurse promptly busied herself getting me set up and showing me that she was happy to make me comfortable there.

Plopping down on my new bed, I began to watch Todd. I wanted to wrap my head around what I was seeing. He began to pull on the IV tube, toy with the machines, and play with them. I asked him to stop, saying that he needed to leave that stuff alone. He just grinned and continued to pull on tubes.

My daughter, Julia, suggested that I ask him if he knew who I was.

"Do you know who I am, Todd," I asked.

"Why, you're Jenny," he said.

Jenny is my daughter. He doesn't know me right now. I'm familiar though.

The nurse popped in and asked her own set of questions. "Where are you?" to which he answered, "Madison." Madison is in Wisconsin. Todd has lived in Arizona for 20 years.

The nurse asked, "What day is it?" and "what month is it?"

He guessed at several answers trying to find one she liked. It looked to me like he had lost 20 years somehow.

The doctors and nurses who came in and out, apparently hoped that I could keep Todd under control but I couldn't. I couldn't stop him from playing with the tubes. They didn't seem worried so I calmed down and breathed to slow down my own angst. There was a flurry of activity and then staff came in and began to package him up for a test. I asked about their plan and said that 'I would' be in on whatever test, scan, or treatment they did. They looked at each other and concluded that I was not going to allow Todd to go anywhere without me. Accepting this outcome, they simply informed me of how things would be done, where we were going, and what gear I had to wear in order to be present, that the machines would be very loud and then,

"Let's go!"

The first test was the MRI and yes, it was loud. I wore a lead apron and watched him be rolled inside a large tube that would help them locate and count the tumors in his brain. Sadly, that test revealed eleven tumors.

The doctor said to me on the phone later, after begging him to tell me the truth;

"He has eleven tumors in his brain, he smoked, there are too many to operate, he can't be saved."

At dinner that day I shared this verdict with my family and friends who had gathered for Todd. Everyone looked at each other wordlessly. There was total silence; you could've heard the proverbial pin drop. The truth was out there now. And we would do what we could do to work with it.

Subsequent tests were set up and finally, he began what was concluded as the best protocol: radiation. He was fitted with a helmet of sorts to wear in each treatment so that the tumors could be targeted with the rays. Two treatments were done and release date was upon us.

I drove Todd to what would become our compound for caring for him until he died. Sybil provided us with a modified mobile of hers that was vacant at the time. I furnished it with furniture from my previous home. Altha, Payton, and I moved in with Todd and began to live a life that unfolded in a brand-new way. Altha and Todd got real bedrooms and Peyton got a narrow hallway by the laundry while I got the sofa bed in the living room.

Previously I had lived in Wheels but had moved into a room at Sybil's just a week before Todd went in for that diagnosis. I moved back out of Sybil's and into Todd's compound when Altha moved in there and expressed fear and worry about handling things alone. I heard her and acted immediately to put myself there.

Todd had been living in an RV and he was now moved to the compound but often he went back to his RV where he felt at home. He had his stash of movies there and it was his 'home.' Peyton lived somewhere else, too, and was now choosing to move here with us. He would prove to be a huge source of comfort for me over time. His innate wisdom and intuition answered many questions I had.

We had reeled off in many directions at that time and none of us was really close geographically or otherwise. We were loosely connected by blood. Loving, nurturing, open and honest, deep and connected; we were not. There was a lot of dysfunction in our home and we all got our own version of it. Hence, none of us ever got to work through our stuff alone or together. Now we were going to dive into something that would require us to live close and deal with the unknown. Where it would lead and what was required of us was all a mystery. But we all jumped right into it, nevertheless. That in itself is very telling of who we were at the core.

We were all pretty similar except Sybil. She was the alpha. She was the favorite and I came to see that once you were that, you never were anything but that. Entitlement was a part of that role and none of the rest of us had the least bit of that notion. The Arizona group, Peyton, Sybil, and I were the team along with Altha who was committed to taking care of Todd.

Our days unfolded in a manner made for reality TV. Altha became the cheerleader, rising every morning, early, chirping to Todd, asking what he wanted for breakfast. In this way I saw her nurturing and loving him in a way I had not seen before. Taking on this project at her age was commendable in my eyes. I was awed by how she did it so bravely with no possible way to understand how it would unfold. Peyton, as it turned out, was more psychic than I

24

knew and during his sleep at night, he dreamt of how it felt to be Todd. He felt the crowded brain and that helped him see, and it helped me see what Todd was going through. I also had the good fortune to witness how Peyton's depth was being exposed to me.

There is no better opportunity, than this, to really see who people really are. It was a crash course in human dynamics, and we all got signed up. I took a week on and a week off, taking turns with Sybil. She took a trip first that was already planned, to Alaska, so the first few weeks it was me on duty. She moved a large RV onto the property for herself, so she had her own space when needed. I chose to be right in the middle of it all so I could keep a closer watch on what went down. I thought that was more comforting to Altha, also.

To begin with, we drove the 90 miles to Tucson twice a week for radiation treatments. The longer they could shrink the tumors, the better chance Todd had to continue living and being 'Todd.' The in-between days we lived life by the seat of the pants. We took turns cooking dinner. Altha loved making casseroles and roasts so that was what she did to feed us. I liked to cook on the grill and so did Peyton, so our meals centered around the grill.

Every night we built a huge bonfire and gathered around it in lawn chairs, drinking cocktails and for some of us, smoking cigarettes or cigars. Goldie, a shy middle-aged neighbor woman, joined us most nights and found comfort in our nightly communing as did Pete, another single neighbor. This was our community and our ritual, and it kept us sane.

Todd was always in the middle of our circle tipping over lawn chairs trying to make sense of them. Peyton said he was trying to make sense of his life. We let Todd smoke when we were close and he could be seen trying to light his cigarette with his phone. Those moments were both sad and humorous and very telling. He seemed to be able to talk to us just fine but was dragging his left leg more and more and his hair was almost gone.

What touched my heart so much was that no matter how he looked, he didn't seem to have an ego, he didn't seem to care about his hair or his new limp. But, when it came to using a cane, that was crossing the line. He refused until he finally had to.

He was the kindest, sweetest, gentlest, and most agreeable guy I ever knew. He had a great sense of humor and was always ready to help who ever asked for it. When he lost his driving privileges due to DWIs, he used a motor scooter that he called his 'Hardly Davidson.' He was a dad with two adult sons, divorced for years from their mom and estranged from those sons.

Because he didn't have a good role model, he had no idea how to be married or be a father. His sons grew up without his guidance. Yet there was a wisdom about him that I never saw until we moved in together. On rides to Tucson, we had to ask him how he wanted his death handled. That was so hard, like admitting that it was true, but he seemed to have already made the decision. He wanted to donate his body to science, to Science Care, an Arizona organization, and he wanted to be remembered as 'himself.' Because we never talked intimately, about anything, doing it now was very difficult. And we really didn't know each other. Superficially we did but what I learned through this process was that I missed knowing Todd for who he was on the inside, what his dreams were, and whether he was happy. Watching him live in a drunken stupor most of his life made me think his life was a waste. I couldn't see the meaning in it from a distance. But it was there.

As days wore on, and the treatments were done, Todd started tripping, falling, and getting more confused. I called the doctor that I got to know on Todd's case and asked if we could get another round of radiation. He said we could not. He said that now we had to contact Hospice and make him comfortable. He said Todd had already lived longer than they expected. We had never asked that question. I guess we chose not to know. I hung up and swallowed hard. Next call went to our local Hospice office. I had stopped in to introduce myself and to inform them that we would one day need their service, on the advice of a close friend, Marsha, who volunteered with them. The day they showed up to begin helping us, I cried fearing that Todd would know he was dying. I think now that he always knew.

We were given a vast array of meds for everything from constipation to sleep meds, morphine, and anti-seizure pills. The nurse took us on as a family and shared everything she knew to gently guide us down this road. And I am so grateful for them being there with us through this ordeal.

Every night was pretty sleepless for me because I slept on a sofa bed in the living room, next to the kitchen. Todd would spend hours foraging in and out of the kitchen cabinets and fridge looking for something. He took out whatever caught his eye and added it to a bowl, mixed it up and then added other ingredients. After a long period of mixing and adding, he sat down to taste the concoction. It was very distasteful, of course, and he soon stood up and walked into his bedroom to sleep. Peyton said that Todd was 'jonesing' for something, either drugs or alcohol or cigarettes, and was trying to figure out what his body was craving. Sleeping wasn't a happy thing for him and I never knew why, and since I was too afraid of overdosing him on sleep meds, I always gave him too little.

The day came when he no longer knew when he had to urinate, and it fell on me to introduce 'depends.' I gingerly walked into his room, holding one in my hand, and said that we had to start using these. He was appalled by that so I told him we were all using them now.

He said, "Well, that's the shits."

I helped him put a pair on and helped him get into his PJs for the night.

Soon his depends got too wet, during the night, and he took them off and either put another one on or put two on or flung them all, soaked, around the room. I walked in one morning to see him naked, sitting on the bed, depends strewn about, and knew I had to get him up on the bed to put a fresh pair on. I asked Peyton to help me. Somehow, I knew that Todd couldn't follow directions. I asked Peyton to take Todd by the upper body and I would take his legs, and we would move him up onto the bed. Peyton grabbed Todd by the wrists, not wanting to touch him, and tried to drag his whole body that way. I was feeling irate like he was going to break Todd's wrists. I yelled at him to take a hold of him lower on his arms. But Peyton was just acting normal. In our family no one was ever seen nude. And we

28

didn't touch each other. It just wasn't done; no hugs and no pats on the back. So, seeing Todd nude was hard for both of us. And I was embarrassed for Todd. Somehow, we managed to move him up enough so I could put new depends on him, then I laid him down, pulled the blankets up to his chin, ran my fingers through his hair and touched his face. I suddenly knew that it was time to touch him and 'love' him. I brought him his nightly pills and asked him to lift his head to take them and a sip of water. He tried to lift his head and could not. He shook so hard it crushed me to see. I held his head and fed him the pills and water like I would to a small child. I was seeing his demise but wasn't ready to face it.

I went outside to sit by the fire. I began to cry and that infuriated Peyton. He was repelled by my sobbing. The more I cried, the more he yelled at me. I said it was time to start touching Todd. We fought viciously and then Peyton went to his room. I sobbed so hard that snot hung from my face to my knees. Altha was there in the circle around the fire but what happened right there had to come out. I was seeing something and though I didn't know exactly what it was, it made me know that things had to change. I wondered how Peyton would be the next morning but he woke up the next day like our fight never happened.

We got up, made coffee like we always did, sat on the little deck that Todd made, facing the rising sun and savoring the coffee. The deck was small so we sat close. I noticed that Todd's eyes were darting back in his head and didn't know what that meant. In no time, like magic, Hospice showed up and as the nurse witnessed Todd's eyes, she told us that if he ever did drugs in the past, he thought he put himself into this place and didn't know how to get out. She said that we did not want to see him suffer like this so we needed to begin giving him morphine.

She left and I realized that it was time to give him his morning meds; as I tried to feed them into his mouth, I saw that he could not swallow or even manipulate his mouth to take them in. He tried but couldn't do it. Not sure what I was seeing but knowing it wasn't good, I sat down to think about what to do. We decided that we should take him inside and asked him to stand up. He couldn't! He could not stand up. Suddenly everything was going away. And so fast. We called for a hospital bed and when it was delivered, Peyton and I took Todd in our arms and carried him inside, putting him in the bed which was placed in the living room now, where we could keep a close eye on him. Peyton now held Todd in a new way without the previous fear of touching him. I covered him up and dripped morphine into the corner of his mouth and he slipped into what must have been a coma. I sat beside him like a sentry, never wanting him to suffer seizures or fear again. The only thing he did early on was twist the blanket up and try to drink it; after that he was out. That whole day I sat there watching for any twitches or signs of seizure. I dripped morphine into the corner of his mouth at the slightest movement. I changed his diaper and Peyton was stunned by how I could do that. It wasn't as if there was an option. It had to be done. It was called caring for and loving Todd.

Sybil came over to take her turn and I left to stay at her house, get ready to process my Top-Secret Clearance with the United States Government, and send my application to Washington D.C. The next day I went to Fort Huachuca in

Sierra Vista, AZ, our Army Intelligence base, and met with the security officer to process the clearance. I turned off my phone out of respect for this process and turned it back on as I left the building. There were several voicemails from Sybil.

They all said, "we lost Todd."

What? How could that happen? How did we lose him? Then I knew. Yep, in just that short time that I left his side, he died. I hurried back to the compound and found him surrounded by people, my family, neighbors, friends, and the Hospice nurse. She was there because Sybil called her when she noticed Todd's breathing change. As the nurse walked in the door, she heard his last breath.

Everyone there had some time to process his death but now it was my turn. I sat on the side of his hospital bed and began to run my hands over him. I ran my fingers through his hair, over his face, touched his eyes, touched his legs and arms, (he was still warm!) and did all this as a way to feel that he was really gone, I guess. I never had this opportunity before, so my behavior was new to me too. I was trying to wrap my mind around him being gone. I cried hard and had no awareness of anyone in the room but me and Todd. I was lost in the loss, crushed by losing him.

Why didn't I see it coming? How could I have missed that he was near death while I was dripping morphine into his mouth? Now I reasoned that the tumors grew and squeezed off his brain stem. His last breath was taken in my sister's presence. Had I realized that he was close to death, I would not have left his side.

In working together for Todd's care, Altha, Peyton, Sybil, and I found a balance that was foreign to us. I learned so much about Peyton and kept a photo journal of our life, so I could look back at the moods and precious moments we walked through like the blind leading the blind.

Todd's body was taken by the local morgue in preparation for his transport to Science Care in Tucson where his body would be used for medical research and the cremains would be shipped to his sons.

Our next step was to plan and carry out a memorial. I had never experienced one, but Sybil seemed to know exactly what to do. She invited everyone she knew who knew Todd. He had lived there either with her or near her for those 20 years, so she knew pretty much all about his life.

She planned a big meal and then suggested that Todd's son Garber and I make up speeches to deliver to those who attended. We did so and found a flow to it. Sybil said that it would have more meaning if I read my speech rather than her do one. As people showed up and the huge living room filled up, I was stunned by how many people came for Todd.

Garber and I sat on the hearth by the fireplace facing the room. I began first, once everyone was seated, feeling small and my voice seemed small, too. After I was done, Garber took over and his speech was so tender that no one could avoid sobbing. I sobbed, feeling the pain in his words. Garber was Todd's oldest son and he had never really had a dad. Todd was so occupied with drinking that he was absent for most of Garber's childhood. And yet Garber delivered his speech with great emotion.

Next one by one, people spoke up about how they knew and loved Todd and how he touched their lives. The outpouring of love for him made me aware of how meaningful and important his life really was. It wasn't a waste like I always thought. Now I was disappointed in myself for never really knowing him and for not having a memorial while he was alive so he could see all the love people had for him. I vowed that in the future, for those I loved and participated in their last days, I would request a pre-memorial of sorts, like a 'going away party.'

Volunteering for Disasters

I joined the Red Cross in Modes, California in 2012. My first attempt at sticking my toe into that world was to join what they call the DAT team (Disaster Action Team). My first assignment was to go to fire calls. I signed up to be available on specific days and if a fire occurred, I would get the call with directions to its location. They 'always' came in the middle of the night and they always occurred in the 'hood.' Modes had a lot of hoods. It's a strange juxtaposition because Modes is known as America's Bread Basket where a majority of the country's vegetables and fruits are grown. It is a valley of very lush soil. And it is home to the world's largest winery, Gallo Wine. This area of the state has many great attractions, such as Yosemite National Park and the Giant Sequoia trees. All this goodness and beauty surrounded it and yet meth and homelessness were two major issues here. Where I come from, a small town in Wisconsin with a population of 7,000, we don't really have a 'bad side of town' or a big drug problem. So, this was new to me. My naivete was glaring in hindsight.

I was driving an '86 4Runner at the time, the kind that had a removable top. And with Mode's desert climate, the top was always off of my car. Even in the middle of the night. Even in the hood. Because I was new and being trained, my job was to 'have my team's back.' In the hood, things happen and my team had to be able to focus on the details of the fire and the condition of the family, and not what was happening behind them. They went to the property where the fire had been and documented the damage done, talked to the family and determined their needs, and then set up a place for them to stay, and offered coupons for food and clothing if they needed it.

At my first fire call, I was drifting around taking in every detail so that I could learn the ropes. Being an empathic person, I soon engaged with the people in the middle of this situation. I stood with my team listening to their discussion and watching their actions when a young boy, about 12-years-old, walked up and asked me to watch his backpack for him.

I said, "Sure," and why wouldn't I? It was extremely heavy but I, nevertheless, carried that thing on my back for a very long time as I wandered about witnessing things.

I stood near a couple cops and a fire marshal as they questioned the young kid. It turned out that he was the grandson of the woman who owned the home that burned. I stepped away suddenly feeling like I was eavesdropping on a private conversation. I lined back up with my team and they were talking about how the grandson had started the fire. It became apparent that he had some mental/emotional issues and was known to have been guilty of starting several other fires. He was an arsonist. At that point I thought about the backpack I was lugging around. What, exactly, was in there? I felt a bit sheepish but gathered the nerve to ask one of my teammates to take it to the fire marshal and explain that it belonged to the grandson.

Later, when I told my son about this caper he gasped. "Oh my god, mom, you were probably carrying around his incendiary materials!!!"

At another fire call I was in the middle of my team watching how things were unfolding and Rob, one of our team, asked me, "Rona, do you want to go inside the house with me and see how damage assessment is done?"

"Sure," I said.

He led me to the door and as he took a hold of the door handle, he whispered, "By the way, this is a hoarding situation."

"Oh," I said.

I never knew anyone who was a hoarder so this was a new idea to me, and I had no idea what to expect. We stepped inside and he pointed to the first room on the left, "Nothing happened here," he said.

I looked at the room and it was a mess. Piles and heaps of magazines, newspapers, and boxes, all strewn about. There was only a narrow passageway wide enough for a small body to pass through.

"Nothing happened there," he said, as he pointed to the room on the right. The same disastrous tangle of items heaped up, nothing in any kind of order.

"Nothing happened here," he said as we found a narrow path down a hallway.

"Here's where the fire was," he pointed as we looked into the last room on the right. The ceiling had a big hole in it where the firemen had to cut through to put out the fire. The back wall was charred black and soaked with water.

What I saw in those rooms where nothing happened was actually more alarming than the room that had been damaged. The piles and piles of stuff stunned me. Magazines, newspapers, and clothes, all heaped up and spread all over the house. If he wouldn't have warned me, I would have thought the firemen made that mess. I had never seen anything like it.

We stepped back outside and walked over to the woman who owned the house. She was sitting on a chair in the middle of a bunch of her neighbors, also sitting on chairs that were fanned out like they were the audience to some kind of show. The homeowner sat there in perfectly neat and clean pajamas, her hair was perfectly rolled up in brush rollers and not a hair out of place. I wondered how this could be the one who lived in that clutter when she looked so immaculate.

My team did their assessments and I stood by watching as a young black boy came up to me and said, "I saved that lady's life."

"You did?" I said.

"Yes," he said, "I saw the smoke coming out of her garage and went to her door and knocked hard on it until she woke up and opened the door."

"Wow, I am so proud of you," I said. "You are amazing and thank you for doing that."

Another time I told my son I was being called to a fire, again in the hood, and he asked to come along to see that it was a safe environment. I gave him the address and we met there. We stood outside a fenced-in yard where it looked like people were having a picnic. There were people sitting in lawn chairs, people meandering about the yard, and toddlers in diapers. The address was right but it didn't make sense that they all would be hanging out in the yard. Just then, Norah, one of our team, walked up and said, "Yep, that is the right place."

My son left and Norah and I walked inside the fence to meet up with the people. First, she talked to an older man who was sitting on a chaise lounge chair. As she talked to him, he pointed to his grandkids running around in diapers, his kids who were the parents, his ex-wife who was pacing around the yard, and then he explained that his wife had a heart attack when she discovered the fire and the ambulance took her to the hospital.

Norah walked off to do something else and I sat down on the end of the chaise lounge chair because he seemed to need to talk. He said that he never could get ahead financially, and that he took care of everyone here and that they all lived with him. And that no one appreciated him or helped him. As he talked, he turned his head to the left and I saw a huge crater on his head.

"Phew," that was a shocker to me.

I swallowed and he said, "Yep, that's where I had a tumor removed."

My mind was busy wondering how so much could go wrong for one guy. I let him vent all that he needed and then Norah came and got me.

She said to me on the way out, "Rona, thank you for doing that, that man needed to talk, and you were a big help by listening to him like that."

Her comments helped me feel like I was being helpful even though I was such a newbie to this work.

At one of the regular meetings with the DAT team they talked about their annual Poinsettia Day. It's an exercise in gift giving where every donor who gave the Red Cross $50 or more dollars receives a big, beautiful plant. They organized teams to make many deliveries throughout the city and I got assigned to work with Bob. Together, we loaded up one of the Chapter's white vans with plants and headed out to conquer the long list of addresses assigned to us.

One by one, Rob drove us to homes and we both went to the door, handed the plants to the people and thanked them for donating to the Red Cross. Rob saved one address for last because it was farther out, in Riverbank, CA. We drove to the neighborhood and found the tiny, humble home.

We looked at each other puzzled and said, "This can't be the one, the owner of this house couldn't have afforded to donate."

But we walked up to the door, anyway, plant in hand, and Bob knocked on the door. After a few hard knocks we walked back toward the van.

Just then we heard a little old lady yelling at us, "Hello, I'm here, it just takes me longer to get to the door because I walk with a cane and am hard of hearing."

We turned around and looked at this little, wrinkled, old gal, with a knit hat pulled down on her head, and walked back to her. We told her why we were there and she invited us in. We followed her inside and handed her the plant and thanked her for donating. She had this forced smile on her face as she asked us to stay a while. While we talked to her, slowly that smile turned to the saddest face we ever saw.

She could no longer keep up the mask. Her name was Natay, she was in her nineties and was so lonely. She needed to talk so we hugged her and sat down to listen to her. She told us how her son died and she was so lonely now. She talked about how she needed a new stove, that her daughter lived far away in Oregon, and just let go of everything on her heart. We hugged her again and I asked if I could take a picture of her. She was so charming with that knit hat and her little wrinkled face despite being hunched over, all full of sadness and longing and that smile long gone.

She said, "Yes" and I took a picture of her and promised to return for visits. When we got back to the office, I told Peg, the Chapter manager, about Natay and she looked through her files to find her donation record. She had not donated at all this year but had donated $20 a year earlier. Peg grinned and said, "It was meant to be."

When we told her about Natay's loneliness, everyone in the office at the time said they would stop and visit her. I did go to see her, always with treats in hand, and often with my daughter or another team member. Every time we tried but it seemed like we could not fill up that empty hole that was her loneliness. I left town soon after that, continuing on with my 'nomadic journey' and when I returned, I found out that she had died. Everyone at the Chapter felt like they didn't visit her enough.

I said, "Don't feel guilty, you visited her as much as you could and so did I."

I was knee-deep in the middle of a 14-year nomadic journey. It was autumn of 2010 and I had just returned to California to visit my daughter, Julia. We had hopped in her car to go to one of our favorite places, Barnes and Noble bookstore. We loved shopping for good books. On our way downtown I got a call from Peg at the Chapter office.

"We have a disaster, run to Maryland because Hurricane Sandy is coming, and they need help. If you want to go, you need to be at the office within an hour."

Wow. I looked at Julia and she said, "Go for it, mom." I told Peg I wanted to go and was thrilled, and surprised at the same time to realize that I was trained enough to go. We went back to Julia's and called my son who lived close by. Those two kids teamed up and, between donating their own stuff and shopping for other items I might need at a military surplus store, my kids packed me up and I was ready within the hour.

Peg and the other office staff took care of all the paper work, got us debit cards, ID's, and information about where we would be and what to do once we landed. We were set up with a flight out of San Francisco at midnight. Pedro and I were the only two going from Modes. Pedro had been on a run before, but he was manic and talked nonstop all the way to the airport. I wanted to duct tape his lips. It was a long one-and-a-half-hour ride and I couldn't even think with his anxious self in that car. We got to the airport and went through the drill to get to our gate, where we met up with other red cross volunteers from different areas of the state, flying in to help with the hurricane. Pedro didn't have the money for his baggage so I paid for it. I thought of it as foreshadowing for what lay ahead. Whatever showed up on this adventure would all be brand-new to me and I'd have to roll with it.

When we landed in Baltimore it was early morning. We were instructed to get a car and call the local headquarters to get instructions. We did and were told to show up ASAP. We walked in and fell into a chaotic crowd of people all trying to do the same thing as we were. All of us trying to get lined up with a place to go and a job to do. We had to get into the Baltimore Chapter system and wait to be assigned a job. It took hours and hours. Some people grabbed stuff that showed up first. Pedro grabbed a job with people he knew from another run so he left right away.

I finally took a shelter in Maryland and was given a motel to stay at and a school that was being used as a shelter. I drove there, unpacked my stuff in my room, and drove to the school. When I got there, a married couple, Harp and Kay and one woman, Sarah, were there. The married couple had envisioned taking the day shift, and giving Sarah and me the night shift. There were soldiers mingling about as support for when the storm rolled in. When Harp and Kay took one look at me and learned that I had not slept for quite a long time, they relented and took the night shift, and let me go back to my motel to sleep. I couldn't sleep though. I was way too stimulated and decided to follow the storm on my computer. I had a 'hotspot' with me so I could get Wi-Fi anywhere. The news was fever pitch about the impending doom and gloom that was Hurricane Sandy. Finally, I got a couple hours sleep and returned to the school. We were there when the storm rolled in. It was ferocious. Rain, wind, and lots of damage along the coast. As time wore on, it was determined that no one was coming to our shelter, so we closed it, and I returned to headquarters to get reassigned.

When people accept a disaster run, they have to promise to stay two to three weeks. I was assigned to a new motel room for the night and a new roommate, Amilia. We were directed to get in touch first thing the following morning for our assignment. No assignment was there for us, so we went to headquarters. Eventually, I noticed on my computer that Red Cross was begging for blood. I thought to myself, *nothing is happening here right now so why not donate blood while I am in a holding pattern?*

I noticed that the building where they were taking blood was right next door. How convenient. I went over and walked in to see what was up. A nurse met me—I was the only one there—and told me that they were only taking 'double red' that day, and went on to describe how it was going to look. It would take three hours as twice the amount of a normal donation would be taken from me. Blood would be drained from one arm, and what looked like beer would be extracted from the blood, and put back into my body through the other arm. Both arms would have to remain stretched out for the entire three hours with me pumping balls every few seconds for the entire time. I would get really cold, but they would cover me with blankets and put a movie on to entertain me.

She described the pitfalls that could show up and at that point I said, "Let's do it, I'll be fine, I always am."

She ran me through the usual intake process and tested my blood. My iron count was high which was a requirement to donate this way. She took me over and had me climb onto a bed/chair apparatus where she began to set me up to donate. Everything she said would happen did. I was quite cold. She said that if I fell asleep and quit squeezing the balls, an alarm would go off. I think it might have happened once. I saw a movie that I'd already seen so asked for another. She put a comedy on and the hours ticked away.

43

When we were done, and I was fine, she told me that we were two people on the same page in life and that I was saving at least three lives by donating my blood.

I walked to the snack table and pulled out my phone to check messages. Since it was turned off, I didn't know that headquarters was frantically trying to get me and had called countless times, and by now they were hot with anger. They were so mad at me for being out of reach that they couldn't contain their anger. They said that I was theirs while I was volunteering for them and that they were responsible for my well-being. I got yelled at and one of the guys was still so mad that he couldn't quite give up on unleashing his anger. Finally, a woman who was assigning volunteers jobs walked up, gave me a hug, and said, "You did the right thing by donating blood."

I felt like crying right then but pushed my emotions aside since I was now in the middle of a whole lot of people. *Who wants to start crying right in the middle of a crowd?*

I was finally assigned to go with Clay, Ranger, Randy, Amilia, and Sarah to New York because they needed more help there. We were directed to go get a maxi van from a rental agency and load up and head for the headquarters in White Plains, NY.

Clay took the wheel first and I rode shotgun. By the time we got to headquarters, everyone knew the first thing they wanted to do is ditch Sarah. She, ironically, was quite like the storm coming in. She couldn't or wouldn't stop talking which made it impossible to hear the GPS and get to our location. Everyone took turns telling her to quiet down but she didn't. When we got to White Plains, the guys ditched us immediately and found a new team to work with. I knew

44

they would. Amilia was beside herself by now wanting to ditch Sarah too. She tried everything she could to get on another team but it didn't happen. Now she was not only with Sarah and me, but Sarah encouraged Pepe and Dana, two innocent bystanders, to join us. Since they were totally unaware of what they were signing up for, they readily agreed to go with us. Amilia was seething.

Now we were five, four girls and one guy. We still had the maxi van. Amilia started off as our driver. She seemed very capable to drive around in Manhattan. She drove and I rode shotgun. We were doing great until someone lightly rear-ended us. She had a meltdown at that point and said she would not drive anymore. That left me. I was seriously the only choice now. I had a hunch this would eventually happen but was more than happy to wait until it was unavoidable.

Driving around in New York City was not for the fearful, and driving a maxi-van in New York City was even more daunting. And having Sarah along was only for the bravehearted. I got in the driver's seat and Amilia took shotgun. She was highly adept at spotting people who were either on their phones, texting, or not paying attention and that even included taxis who were ferociously pushing to get ahead of us. If we had an inch, she would tell me, "GO!!!"

And I would. We edged out taxis quite regularly which felt pretty good after a while.

We boldly drove around that city just like pros. Finally, we were given shelter in a school on Long Island and headed there. By now all the power was out in the area. There were no house lights, no street lights, just lots of rain

45

and more rain. Stopping at stoplights was on the honor system. Finding our school was hard because GPS didn't work and we went in circles until Amilia spotted an ERV (Emergency Response Vehicle) parked near a shopping center. She jumped out and asked them to guide us. They got us to the school and we walked in to discover that the school was already well staffed. We spent the night there on cots in a gymnasium and waited for our next assignment.

We were sent to a few more schools and always found them to be well staffed. Finally, we were sent to a ship. When we located it, anchored to a pier, we hauled all our stuff up a long, long pier, up a few sets of stairs; and found the bunk room and people who would direct us as to where the bathrooms were for girls, where our bunks were, where we would eat and then left us to settle in. We looked at the bunk beds and thought we knew what we were doing when we each picked out our beds. But getting in and feeling sandwiched in them changed our viewpoint on what was a good choice and what was not. Pepe almost fell out of his bed but Sarah caught him in time to push him back in. I found that the beds were so tight that I couldn't pull my knees up comfortably to read. There was a light, which was good, and blankets. But getting in and out was a handful. The next morning, we all decided that the lower bunks were a smarter choice. We got our beds made up in the lower bunks as a reporter came and wanted to interview me about our jobs. Then we were advised that we were assigned to another shelter closer to the storm.

As we drove, the weather was turning more and more vicious as Hurricane Sandy came up the shore and tore things up. We headed out and now we were four. Amilia

46

begged the ship's officer to let her stay there. She was untreated bipolar, Pepe was treated bipolar and Sarah, well, we were never sure what was up with her. So, I assumed having one less complicated personality could only improve the situation. Dana always made a point of getting the farthest seat in the van, so she felt she was safer there. I drove through the storm, snow, and slush, the wind fiercely blowing, trees falling into the road and limbs breaking off, small branches flew into our windshield, and at five miles an hour, I inched us toward our shelter.

Hours went by and we were pretty silent, full of fear and dread, hoping not to get in an accident because even though the storm was awful, there was still traffic. Anything over five mph and the van fishtailed. And that was far too scary. I spotted a Starbucks on my left and honestly, you'd have thought I saw a million bucks. I drove up and we all headed in for a much-needed reprieve. We all ordered whatever we longed for and when we got out our debit cards, the staff informed us that our order was on them. They were glad we were here to help them and they wanted to cover the cost as well as give us almost everything on their counter that was available. We left feeling renewed and drove on, soon spotting the sign over the highway that named our destination town. *Oh my god!!! Hours and hours had passed with us all in this white-knuckled ride.*

When we finally pulled in, our van was not a pretty sight. It was caked in snow with branches and leaves sticking out of the grill. We walked in to say hello, and the staff told us that they had been following our progress and had been worried about us. Again, I was not expected to cover a shift at first but was able to sleep. The others took different night shifts and we did our best to settle in.

The first night I slept in a cot in what looked like the kitchen. The next day everything was changed up and we slept in the auditorium. But it was freezing cold in there so some chose to sleep in hallways or smaller rooms. It was all very random.

I was the driver to start with because we brought the only vehicle that the shelter had. Not sure how that happened but it did. I drove one guy to the eye doctor, drove others to the train station to go to the city, and rode along with soldiers in their hummer to grocery shop. That was quite the experience, shopping for a shelter I had just arrived at. One soldier looked at me and said, "Be careful, the Hummer doors are really heavy."

I said, "I know, I've driven Hummers before."

He took a double take and then climbed in for the drive to the store. We shopped with the help of our shelter manager, Joan, giving us approximate quantities of each item. Back at the shelter, I was given the job of registering people who wanted to stay at the shelter. That job turned out easy because no one wanted to stay in a shelter. They would rather stay in their freezing houses than leave and have someone ransack their home of all their beloved stuff.

One by one, however, people did come in to eat or talk. One lady came in and was very lively. She ended up telling us about the Rockettes playing in Manhattan, near Radio City, and knew a number to call to get cheaper tickets. She was a beauty, fun to talk to, and full of life and information. She left and a couple who were newly married came in. They both had cancer. Hers was under control due to an alkaline diet and she was trying to heal him with the same diet. When they left then came a guy in his eighties. He wanted food for himself to eat there and then food to take home to his wife who was staying at the house to protect it. I took him to the kitchen and sat down with him as he enjoyed the meal I placed in front of him. I said that I just wanted to sit with him and hear his stories. He was surprised but shared a bit before asking about me. I said that I was a nomad, didn't have a home, and was traveling around the country and the world for years.

He said, "Well, that's different."

I grinned to myself. Few people could understand that way of living. Especially those who prize their home. He finished up and took a plate of food home to his wife.

The team and I sat together, and talked about who wanted what day off soon and as everyone picked,

I said, "I don't care, where the heck am I going to go on my day off anyway?"

I took the last choice of days and so did Joan; we would share our day off. I got tickets to the Rockettes for her and myself, and before long, we learned that our shelter was closing. We had two people in it at the time. A homeless guy and a lady who was agoraphobic, whose brother got her out of assisted care and brought her there to be safe. We moved them to another shelter and now we were done.

My time was up, and we could either stay on or go home. Sarah, Dana, Pepe, and I drove back to Manhattan and got a room in a hotel in Upper Manhattan. Our headquarter was now moved to another area of town. Our rooms were donated by a professional sports team who had planned to stay there but gave up their rooms for us.

I got my team flights back to their homes and stayed one more day to see Ground Zero. Everyone would be staying one more day and I would be staying two more.

I took off on a subway train headed for the direction of Ground Zero with the advice of the staff in the hotel. I rode to the end of the line expecting the conductor to announce Ground Zero's stop. But it wasn't called Ground zero. It was called Chambers Street. At the end of the line we were told to get off, it was the end of the line.

I told the guy, "I'm trying to get to Ground Zero."

He said, "Get on this train, get off here, get on another train, get off there. And then walk to it."

I got back on the train heading the other direction and the train was packed. Immediately a man jumped up when he saw I was Red Cross and gave me his seat. I was awed by that! I got to the end where I had to get off to see Ground Zero. I turned my phone GPS on and walked to the site. Once inside, I wanted to walk around, feel the energy there, take some pictures and rest, and just absorb what happened there. I took a couple pics, read some of the names along the edge of each pool, and sat down for a breather. On the loud speakers I heard an announcement, "We are closing in 30 minutes."

Oh damn!!! All that work to get here and now I have to leave. I still felt thrilled, firstly that I actually got here and got to see some of it, and secondly, I was pretty dang proud of feeling brave enough to wander up and down in New York City without fear. Now it was time to return to the subway. I walked to one station, walked down two flights to the ticket office, which was closed, and there was no way to get on that train. Back up two flights and down the side walk to another subway station. *Nope, that one didn't work either.* Finally, I spotted a man in a booth that looked like an information booth. I asked for help. He directed me up another block to the train that would take me back to my hotel. By the time I got on that train and seated, a woman sat next to me. She was totally twisted up with worry over her son getting a sex change and wanted to vent to me. I was more than happy to let her do that if she would just tell me when to get off at my stop. She said she would but as she deep-dived into her story I didn't trust her, so I busted in over and over and asked, redundantly, "Is this my stop coming up?"

"Nope," she said as she went on pouring out her pain. I butted in again and again, frantic about getting lost. Finally, my stop came, and I said goodbye and marched off, totally out of breath and euphoric over looking at my hotel just across the street. You could have given me a thousand dollars and it wouldn't have thrilled me more.

I walked into my hotel, and my team was all standing around and waiting for me to go to dinner. It would be our last time together. They said they picked a place across the street. *Thank the gods!!! I couldn't have gone much further.* We walked over to Pete and Johnny's Restaurant and asked for a table. With our Red Cross garb on, we got immediate attention. We were led upstairs to a table. *Oooooh, I am so tired of stairs!* But up we went. We sat down and looked at the menus. We took off our Red Cross vests and lanyards, per protocol, and I ordered a glass of wine; my first since coming on this adventure. We knew that the Red Cross frowned on drinking with our Red Cross items on; it was our last day and we had no more responsibility. Excited to be sitting down, drinking wine, and about to eat, I said, "Okay, tell me, one by one, something I don't know about you."

When the words came out, I thought, *how dumb is that!* Of course, I know nothing about any of them other than our time here. But, ironically, they all responded just as though they never saw the weirdness in that statement at all. We ordered dinner and enjoyed being together for our last night, and for really getting a chance to talk about ourselves.

The next morning everyone was off to their flights home. I had the day to sight see and chose to take a tour bus—a double decker—on a tour of Upper and Lower Manhattan. I rode in the upper deck thinking; *It would be the best view*. The upper deck had a plastic protection barrier surrounding the first two feet and the rest was all open air, and it was freezing out. I so wanted to do this so I toughed it out as the guide announced that we were passing Yoko Ono's condo, how she burned her brains out with drugs and couldn't take care of herself anymore, and the first cancer hospital, Central Park, and so on before returning.

It was time to change to another bus for the Lower Manhattan tour. I couldn't make myself freeze anymore and didn't want to get sick, so I opted to go to my room, snuggle into bed, and journal about my experience. Then I got dressed and walked across the street to that same restaurant for dinner. I was given a seat at the bar this time. I was thrilled, happy to be warm and comfortable. I happily ordered a glass of wine and a meal. The bartender needed to vent about her life in New York, about her mother, and about how hard it is to find good jobs. I let her because, why not, this was almost the theme of the trip at this point. The more she talked, the more grateful she felt, and she bought me a glass of wine. *Ah, that was a real gift.* I had dinner and walked out of there feeling like New Yorkers were normal just like the rest of us.

The next morning, I walked kitty-corner to a diner for breakfast. I had biscuits and gravy with lots of fresh hot coffee. *Yes, happiness.* As I walked back across the street, I could hear someone yelling something. Not sure what though. I listened.

"Red Cross lady, Red Cross lady!!!" I turned and there standing in the road was a guy, wanting to thank me for coming to help them and wanting to shake my hand. *Whoever thought New Yorkers were cold and unfriendly??? Not on my watch!!!*

I flew home that afternoon, a long, long flight all the way from one coast to the other. I thought I would never get there. When I did, guess who picked me up in San Francisco? Pedro. He had come home early and was preparing for another run. This time he was quiet and took me to my daughter's and dropped me off. What a whirlwind of an adventure. No one could make this stuff up!!!

Crossing into Belize Illegally

My partner, at the time, Miles was a handful. He was one of those people who come into a girl's life for a season. I knew of many women he had spent time with and it seemed as though his path was a rocky one, though he wanted to believe he had all his ducks in a row. It was a four-year-long stretch with him, after my seven year stretch with a farmer, and that followed many short terms and the 28-year-long marriage. That has been my path. Rocky, also.

What happened in those four years with Miles was a lot. A lot of adventure, a lot of learning, a lot of pain, and a lot of growth. I learned from my partners, but I couldn't help it if they did or didn't learn from me.

Miles had a dream. He wanted to retire in Belize. He didn't tell me about it until the end when he knew it was a bad idea. I thought he was just angling for another adventure. At the time of this plan he was concocting, he was 64 and I was 62.

He found a website that offered caretaking opportunities all over the world. All of them required you to get there and then you could live free in their house, farm, ranch or whatever, while they ran off on an adventure. You get to take care of things and they leave. You get an opportunity to experience a different way of life and they get a break from their life. It sounded right up my alley. The adventure, that is.

Miles found an opportunity in Belize, Central America, an organic fruit and flower farm called We Can Do It. Yolanda and Roman owned the farm. They had once been very successful business people in Hawaii and California but then they decided to change up their life. They wanted something with more 'meaning.' They bought the farm (and as you'll see later this wording is perfect) and left their old way of life. Their farm house was on legs, surrounded by a moat and the farm was in the jungle, for real.

Miles started communicating with Yolanda and Roman via email, and after a few days, we signed up to go there and caretake their farm. In fairness, they tried to warn us what was 'normal' life there but it didn't sink in.

They said, "Biting bugs."

We knew biting bugs, I lived in Wisconsin where our native bird was the mosquito. In Arizona where we lived now, there were a ton of venomous biting things.

They said, "Lots of rain."

Who doesn't know about monsoon season? Arizona has it for about six weeks. None of that scared us off.

We packed up and got ready for the road trip from El Paso, Texas to Belize through all of Mexico. As we were tying up loose ends, Miles pulled out his passport and saw that it had 'CANCELLED' written across it. When he got it back from the courts (he was delinquent in child support in Wisconsin), he never noticed that. Now he could not legally cross into Belize.

But I could and I bravely said, "Well, I'm going anyway."

At that time, I was pretty much sick of him. I was finding that life with him wasn't that much fun anymore.

He said, "I'll figure it out when we get there."

"Okay," I said.

Over dinner that week, we talked about this long drive through Mexico and all of our Arizona family said, "Don't do it!!! We'll never see you again!!!"

We knew of one area of Mexico that was dangerous, Chiapas, and would avoid it but otherwise we looked at this with zero fear.

We got all kinds of warnings. Never drive after dark, don't drink the water, you could get kidnapped, and watch out for food poisoning, (the green apple two-step).

We drove over the border and Miles had an idea where he wanted us to stay, and he wanted to mingle in each city to get to know the culture a bit. Every city seemed to have a central park which was perfect for observing their culture. We headed down the eastern side of the country, stopping our first day at Gomez Palacio, 500 miles from El Paso. Next, we headed for San Luis Potosi. This is where all the warnings about getting speeding tickets if we were on the roads after dark, became true. We couldn't find a motel for anything, it was getting dark, and along came an officer. He pulled us over, I was driving. He said we were speeding and that we had to pay $140 American Dollars. I saw his ticket book in his back pocket. He never brought it out. He had no plans to. He was doing exactly what we were told they did.

Everyone had their own warnings.

Some said, "Demand to go to the police department and fight it."

But the funny thing is that when you're actually in the moment, it's dark, and you kind of know that it would not work, you just go ahead and freaking pay that money to the man. After that, knowing full well that he was off with our money ready to have a good time, we continued looking for a motel.

We came across one and drove up to a few men sitting beside a table at the entrance to a parking area. That was unfamiliar.

We said, "We wanted a room."

They said, "For how many hours?"

What, I thought? *A night's worth, just saying!* But it turned out that this place was set up for trysts and men reserved rooms for just a roll in the hay. Miles called it a 'no-tell-motel.' It was definitely my first rodeo. They pointed out to a place to park my car and when I pulled in, they raced to pull a curtain behind my car. *That's odd!!!* We went inside and found nude pictures on the walls and the TV had nothing but porn movies on it. In the wall, there was a turntable where you order food, it is brought to that turntable, you put your money on it and turn it out, and the food is put on and the money taken off.

The windows were very high and heavily curtained. It was clear that this was a very clandestine situation. And the funny thing was that at one point I heard some yelling outside. A woman had found her husband shacking up with another woman and there was a whole hell of reckoning to be done there.

Miles seemed to be aware of these places but for me, it was pretty disgusting. In the morning we were awakened by the phone; we were being alerted that our time was up. I probably could have lived without that adventure.

Next on our stops was Vera Cruz. When we drove into town, the ocean was right there and it smelled like sewer. I tried to wade in the ocean but my mind kept telling me that the smell had to be coming from the water so I couldn't get past my shins. We went to dinner at a restaurant beside the sea and what we would usually do in the states is ask for a glass of water. Miles did that without thinking. If the smell here was like sewer, my thought was, *don't drink the water!!!* He didn't ask for purified water and when the waitress brought the glass of water, I looked at it thinking, *Hmmm, doesn't look all that clear to me.*

He drank it down during dinner and before long the shit literally hit the fan. He had the 'green apple two-step' and it wasn't so funny for him. I, on the other hand, kind of smirked to myself thinking, *how could you miss that the stink here is sewer!!!* Even the locals don't drink the water.

As we lingered in the central parks of some of these cities, we people-watched and because we were a real anomaly there plus the fact that I had yellow hair at the time we were seriously stared at. But I am a great one to stare at people; I just love to study them.

Miles had a rough ability to speak their language and I had about a dozen words in my bilingual cache so when we sat down, looked at a menu and ordered breakfast, for example, we ordered different things but got the same thing. I saw this as being like Forrest Gump's Box of Chocolates. You never know what you're going to get. I know that with my hand signals and attempts to get my choice across to them, they tried hard to figure me out. It didn't matter so much to me what we got as long as I could tell what it was. But one time, I ate their stewed beans and loved them, yet they made my body revolt. I wondered what the heck could be in them that would make my gut explode. Some said they use lard to add flavor. I would have to skip that delicacy in the future.

I am no prima donna but as we stopped at banos (bathrooms) along the way, they didn't have toilet paper and I resented that, but then the toilet seats disappeared! That was just rude! But you know what they say, "When in Rome, do as the Romans do." Mmmmhmmm.

When we were close to Mexico City, we had an idea it would be a major chaotic mess to drive through there, so we asked a policeman for advice on how to 'go around it.'

He said, "Oh, go right through, it is the best way!"

So, we did. It turned out to be my turn at the wheel. As I inched through that city, I was stunned by all the action. People, kids, bikes, animals, and people encroaching the 'topes,' presenting their wares for sale, buses, and trucks. And their speed bumps were alarmingly more like 'ski jumps.' All in all, it was a major conglomeration of life. I took a deep breath and decided to 'do what they do.' I bravely drove right through that city without fear and dodged everything, winding my way through it all, just like the locals do.

As I was leaving, I noticed that there was no aggression there. Miles called it their 'wah,' their energy. They were all just happy campers doing what they do. No aggression. It made all the difference. As I was on the outskirts of the city heading down a two-lane road, the cars on both sides swooped onto the shoulders so that we could have a four-lane road. It was all good and everyone made it work. I thought that was way cool! Mexico City was just fine to drive through.

In Cancun we spent time on the beach at a resort, sunbathing and enjoying the beauty for a few hours, then visited Tulum, a Mayan ruin on the sea. It is the only ruin built right on the edge of the sea. Then we moved on down to the Yucatan and checked out Chichen Itza. It is very famous and a very spectacular Mayan ruin. I loved it and was mystified by the whole idea of these temples, and why the Mayans no longer used them.

As we neared Belize, we stayed at a resort just this side of the border, in Chetumal. The owners sat with us and socialized and warned us, "You do not want to go to Belize! Those people are no good!"

I admit, it made me laugh. It's like the trickledown thing. We, as a culture, tended to look down on the Mexicans, they looked down on the Belizeans, and later we discovered that the Belizeans looked down on the Guatemalans. Then I thought, *Geeze, do the Canadians look down on us???*

This was where Miles had to conjure up a plan to get himself over the border to Belize. We drove to the little area near the border gate and guardhouse. He watched boats come and go and laid a plan to ask a boat owner to drive him across that little stretch of water. He said he would say that he was going over to have lunch and would return. I was a mere witness to all this. He asked a guy named Providentia, and the guy said, "Sure."

He promised to meet Miles at the pier the next morning early. Michael thought that name was a good omen. But, Providentia didn't show. Michael tried another boat owner. This time the guy was willing to take him right then. He climbed into the boat and as I stood there watching, the Immigration Officer walked onto the pier, hands on his hips, frown on his face, asking in a gruff voice, "What is going on here?"

Miles sold him his story and the guy bought it. Now Miles was gloating over pulling off this coup. He hunkered down feeling real good about himself and the boat motored away toward the little bay of Corozal, and Smuggler's Den, the resort he was aiming for.

In true keeping with how Miles works, he left with no concern for how I would manage the border crossing on my own; a woman, yellow hair and all, crossing into Belize alone. I didn't give it any thought either! And I'm the one who suffered!!!

The guards did not buy it. They looked at me and decided that something was up with this plan. They would not believe a woman would travel across country alone like that. They searched my glove compartment, trunk, all of our luggage and here is where the catch showed up. I was not a good liar and I didn't hatch a plan for how to pull this off. It was my first rodeo so I had no idea how it would play out. When the guards pulled out Miles's skivvies and shaving kit they said, "This is not yours!"

What could I say? I had to lie. If it wasn't for the fact that there was indeed no one hiding in my car, they would not have let go me through. I lied but no one would believe

I wore men's skivvies and had a shaving kit. That was just stupid.

The guard stamped my passport and then directed me to go across the street to get my car sprayed, maybe Belize doesn't want any cooties coming in from Mexico. After the guy sprayed my car, with me in it, he shocked me by hopping in my car. I stared at him wondering, *What the heck!!!*

He said, "Oh, I'll just help you turn your dollars into Belizean money."

"Hmm, okay."

So, he told me where to go; the place was right next to the guard house. Then he stayed in my car. I approached the guards to cross and he stayed right there! They eyed him, he eyed them, and I wondered what was said there. They let me pass. I almost held my breath wondering what his plans were. Then he told me to pull over and let him out. He jumped out at the edge of the road and I had a 'come to Jesus' moment right then. I was so unprepared for this whole crossing deal that happened that I didn't know what to do about. Looking back, I think that guy rode through the check point to see that I really was alone.

Now to find Miles. It seemed logical to keep following the land as it swung back toward the water. Smuggler's Den, where Miles said he was heading for, had to show up sooner or later, so I drove slowly, hoping to spot a sign. A mile or so down this road I saw a sign laying in the tall grass on my left. I breathed a sigh of relief and headed into the driveway ready for a break. I found Miles gloating, having a meal and a drink, and celebrating his bravado. I was ready for a drink and food too. I was pissed off that he was acting all proud of himself with no concern for how my crossing went. That was Miles in a nutshell. And look at me, I was so far from realizing and taking my power back, and standing up to behavior like this that I let it pass.

The way I grew up, with no one talking to one another; I struggled with how to relate, confront, and stand up for myself. I was very early into this journey of discovering my power. It would come but at this point I tolerated very poor behavior like that.

As I ate and drank my wine, I breathed a sigh of relief. One more hurdle crossed. Now Miles was getting all antsy about fearing officers would come looking for him. He wanted to skedaddle but I wouldn't do it. Not yet. Time for a moment of applauding myself for getting through that crossing fiasco. As they say in Mexican, muy malo (very difficult).

When we did take off, we headed straight for Orange Walk, just inside Belize, and Miles picked an out of the way hotel, D Elizabeth's and asked me to hide the car in the back. He was still freaked out. Kind of funny, actually.

We meandered down the little country of Belize, end for end, passing curious little villages called, Double Head Cabbage, More Tomorrow, Gentleville, Caves Branch, and Ringtale; and arrived at We Can Do It early afternoon, a few days early. There were bamboo poles across the road with a sign hanging from one, a loose dog prowling the property, and two dogs barking, chained tight. We followed the worn path of the loose dog through the jungle and found our new summer home. No one was home so we unloaded our gear into a side-less shed, and sat down to eat peanut butter/honey sandwiches and smoke a cigar to celebrate making it.

Since no one was home, we drove back to Punta Gorda, the larger city on the sea, and got a room at the See Front Inn, had dinner at Grace's and watched Titanic there while sipping Pino Coladas and Cuba Libres. It felt good to be here. To have come this far with no real tragedies. We explored PG town while hoping to find out where Yolanda and Roman went.

Back at the farm the next day, still no Yolanda and Roman. This time Miles and I asked around the little nearby village of San Pedro, Columbia, and then returned to the farm and parked to walk to the neighbors, the Jasons, to ask them if they knew anything. Sly and Terry invited us in for Kool-Aid. They had a friend visiting, Mr. Tayl, a Jehovah Witness, from nearby Big Falls. We sat in the hardpacked dirt yard on folding chairs, sipping Kool-Aid while Sly pointed to the shed where his wife was cooking up a pot of split peas and pork feet soup. He said that they always had beans; red beans, black beans, brown beans, or peas, and while we sat there, she ran to Columbia, two miles away, on foot, for ice cubes for our drinks. *How did she do it?*

I laughed to myself about the idea in the states of free-range. Everything here was free-range. The chickens, pigs, whatever they had, was free-range. It seemed funny to me. No fences here. Mr. Tayl gave us a ride back to our car in his truck. We stood in the back, holding on to the headache rack and I got a much-needed adjustment on that ride. The roads are hard to describe but hardpacked, potholed, roughly sums it up. One hole connects to the other, so it was uncomfortable riding.

We walked back into the jungle to check on Yolanda and Roman and found them home. They greeted us warmly, and we sat in their screened area under the house to share stories and drink water collected from rainfall, off the roof. It runs into a tank and is then filtered through a couple screens. Some is for drinking, some for showering, and some for watering Yolanda's plants. Roman made a shower in the yard by propping a big tank on a wood frame above a frame for standing in. It was completely open. You open the hose and pour water over yourself and get an open-air shower.

Yolanda made dinner of cucumbers in vinegar broth, rice, and ground beef, crumbled and juicy. We were happy and had full bellies. We were shown our room, a small area lined on three sides with screened windows and a bed made of four-inch foam on slats on a frame, and there was one shelving unit. Shower curtains hung over each window. Bare bones.

After chatting into the evening as vampire bats flew over our heads (on the upstairs veranda), it began to storm, and we retired to our tiny room. The intensity of the rain was shocking to me. When I thought it rained hard, it got harder and harder until I wondered if the roof could hold up under it. The free-hanging shower curtains blew straight out, allowing the rain in onto the luggage lining the walls. Miles braced chunks of wood on the bottoms of the curtains to keep the bulk of the rain out and we moved all our stuff to one corner of the room to keep it dryer. It was hard for me, one who can sleep through anything, to sleep through the pounding rain. It's one thing to know rain and another to know jungle rain. It's a whole different animal. So, this was May 15, our expected day of arrival, and Yolanda and Roman also mentioned that it also happened to be the beginning of their monsoon season. And it was right on time.

Miles got right into the experience first thing. He went to the shed, started the generator, and grounded our coffee beans for our morning coffee. Our favorite thing is coffee beans freshly ground, and coffee made in a French Press. Yolanda and Roman had already gone off to work somewhere on their property of twenty acres.

In our introduction to jungle life, we learned that boa constrictors, scorpions, tarantulas, fire ants, fer de lance snakes, and termites also live here. Good to know. Somehow a frog got up to the second story and into our room right off the bat. Nothing like getting exposed to the real deal right away.

Yolanda showed me the laundry process. The washer, run off a gas-powered generator, does a handful of items at a time. Then after six minutes of agitating, you had to squeeze each item and drop it into a five-gallon bucket of clean rinse water with softener added. Swish those things around and hand squeeze out some water. Next, place them in the spinner where almost all the water is forced out. Then hang stuff on her lines in the yard with clothespins. If it weren't for the fact that the air is drenched, already with moisture, those clothes could dry. It almost felt like hanging your wet clothes in the bathroom after a shower and expecting them to dry.

Miles decided to make a special dinner for Y and R so we shopped in PG town for all the ingredients for his Chicken Cacciatore and a big salad. Next, we found in nearby San Pedro, Columbia, a school that was set up with computers for local use as well as for the school kids. Denys, a Peace Corps volunteer stationed at the school was very interactive with us. She told us about the University of Indiana donating all the computers for the kids here. Then she told about taking her rowboat across the river to get to the school from where she was staying and how she saw a fer de lance snake swimming across the river, too. She told us about bites all over her that she called red bug bites, after talking about the fer de lance snake (one of Belize's most aggressive), and then mentioned other venomous snakes, and the worst one of all, the bushmaster, whose fangs can be up to one inch long. Man, that's more then I want to know. Dang, already jungle life is sounding disgusting.

Back at the farm, Miles prepared an excellent dinner and we tried out the local Belikins beer. R gave us the grand tour of the property showing us where all the organic fruit trees are and that it is up to us to eat up that fruit. He showed us where herbs grew wild that we could use for cooking. He introduced us to the machete that he uses to cut down the tall grass and for other things we don't want to think too much about. He has a mower he demonstrated and said we could mow the lawn now and then. I took one look at the lawn. The way it sunk in when I walked on it seemed more like marsh land. I wondered to myself, what lurks underneath all that thick grass. Our second day was coming to a close and so far, so good.

The next morning, we all took a bus to PG town where Y and R showed us around a bit. There was an internet café (vital for our connection to the real world), a good East Indian restaurant, we learned who to get a boat ride to

Guatemala from, where to purchase secondhand clothes, and who to change money with. We met a local Mayan woman from a nearby village, who at the age of 42, has eleven children. She told us about her husband getting bitten by the fer de lance and said people usually don't survive its bite, but her husband was being treated by a witch doctor who told her, "Do not look at your husband's leg or it will not heal." He had to sleep in a room curtained off from view.

When we got back to the farm, Y made us a dinner of red potatoes, chicken in gravy, and a huge salad and wine. Day three down.

Day four on the farm. We drove to San Pedro, Columbia, and walked to Lubaantun (lube-ban-tune), a Mayan Ruin; a mile and a half out of town. We meditated by an altar there, walked all around the ruins, and got to know the docent, Sango, a bit. He gave us a lot of the background info on the Mayans there and the ruins' history. Sango told us that his elders don't share their wisdom with the new generations. His mother told him that to do it would be like "making herself naked in front of him."

Day five, Y, Miles, and I drove to Stann Creek and the Hane Farm (shrimp farm) where Emma and Heron, friends of theirs, reside along with all of the workers (ten or more). It is a big operation. Two gals work in the kitchen all day, making meals to feed all the workers, staff, one biologist, and the family. They have twelve shrimp ponds. We walked by the ponds and I got a real idea of how farm raised shrimp look in those pools. Emma and Heron treated us to lunch with them and their gang. Deep fried, marinated and coated shrimp, spinach, salad, rice, broccoli bread, banana bread, and iced tea were served. No wonder those two gals are kept busy. That's a lot of food for lunch.

We left for a tour of San Ignacio and Santa Elena. We stayed at the Aquada Hotel and people-watched, noting that a lot of Garifuna populate this village. Garifuna are a people of African and American descent that live mainly along the Caribbean coast of northern Central America—they're also called Black Carib. Them and the Mayans are largely what live in the villages between Stann Creek and Santa Elena. We chatted with a brother and sister from Vail, Colorado, who were backpacking in Belize. They said that when they were backpacking in Peru where she volunteered in the past, she was shown the spiders that will bite you if you don't completely cover yourself with netting and tuck it under you. She described the size and it looked like 'dinner plate,' size to me! Because I have a huge fear of spiders, those stories come right to me.

We headed for another ruin, wanting to see every one we could while we were there, and got off track and a local, Owl, jumped right in the car and directed us right to it. He is a retired government worker. That's real downhome friendliness, I'd say! Driving around the area, we passed Silk Grass, Teakettle, Blackman Eddy, Bullet Tree Falls, Duck Run, Spanish Lookout, Billy White, Cool Shade, and a creek named Haul Creek. Gotta love those names!

After breakfast the next morning we drove to a ferry in San Ignacio that took us across the creek by a pulley system operated by the driver (like a raft and a pulley), we got to the other side and walked a mile uphill to a ruin called Xunantanich (shun-an-ton-itch). We walked and climbed all over the ruins. For me, it is essential to be able to touch, see up close, and feel the energy of a place and that this was allowed was perfect for me. I loved hiking to the top of the temples and sitting there trying to imagine how this was all built and why. I envisioned the Mayans, like ants, working up and down those temples, building first one and then 13 years later, building another over the top of that one. I thought it was the leader's way of keeping them busy and out of trouble.

While there, we met a couple who were considering going to Caracol, in Guatemala, which was considered absolutely crazy. Whole busloads of people were getting stopped by men who came out of the jungle with machine guns and robbed and raped the people. We wanted to see the ruin there but not that bad.

At the top of the temple we were at, soldiers stood armed with rifles, so I'm good with this. I love risks but not insane ones. We had dinner at Hannah's, run by a Brit expat. The food was East Indian and delish. Then we bought cigars and sat in a park in the center of town and watched the action and smoked our cigars. Life was good.

Still returning from Stann Creek, and stopping along the way to smell the roses, we settled in Dangriga, and got a room at Pal's Guest House. We learned that Garifuna settled here in the 1800s after leaving Africa to start anew. We heard Dangriga-style reggae music being played by a band nearby. People swayed to the beat of the drums. Pretty gals with their babies, older women, men, kids on bikes, all gathered to enjoy the event which looked like their version of a fair. There was one chicken stand at the event. Against the sound of the music, the thunder of the waves rolling up during high tide competed. The fresh ocean air flowed in and it all felt stimulating. We dined early at the only restaurant in town that was open, a Chinese establishment where a local guy joined us and chatted Michael up about sports and shared a Belikin with us. To complete this day, we strolled along the beaches looking for shells and other keepsakes.

On down to Mayan Center Town, we had breakfast at Nu'uk Che'il. Ernest made beans, scrambled eggs, toast, and coffee, and we got to know his wife. She is Mestizo (Spanish Maya). She shared her knowledge and beliefs about the ruins with us. She said they were not homes, not where the Mayans lived, but where they held ceremonies, worshipped and held rituals—like our churches—and they are still used today for such purposes. We never saw that but I like to think it is true.

Placencia was next. It is a small island off of Belize. We waded in the ocean there a bit but as I watched, I noticed that all the locals sat at another part of the beach, near an outlet and as I wondered why, I noticed a cruise ship docked near us and I saw something draining out of the bottom of it. Now I had a feeling that the locals knew that where we sat was not clean ocean water. That planted a thought in my head along with the general feeling of discomfort I felt there. We ate breakfast, soaked up sun and read on the veranda of our hotel. I just don't like the feel of this place for some reason. I couldn't connect to anything or anyone here. It worked for Miles though. He found his people here. It is often that way. What works for him doesn't work for me or vice versa. At this point we have been in Belize for eleven days.

On our way back to PG town, we had breakfast at Café Hello and lunched in PG at Emorys waiting for Supauls to open, which is like a general store where we can get groceries, do email, get boots, and then off to the farm for real. I bought my first eggs there and thought it was odd that the eggs were kept on shelves, unrefrigerated. (I would later discover, when I cracked a couple for breakfast, that they ran out like snot, very runny and disgusting). Y gave us a final walkthrough of where the herbs, spices, fruits and veggies, and flowers grow. It seems simple but in twenty acres, grass up to your waist, jungle and a whole lotta trees and stuff, it is hard to find anything. When R showed us where to dump garbage in the jungle, our first day, we never found that spot again, ever. We had to make a new dump site.

A tutored us on how to take care of the dogs. Sadly, he saw them as only protection for the property, not pets, so they were kept on short chains and looked psycho to me. I would end up thinking of the ways to set them free to live happy lives but also knew that if I got close to them, they could chew me up in a flash. Only one dog was friendly and was allowed to roam freely. Probably why it was friendly. I tried to make friends with the chained dogs but was too afraid to get close. Y made us dinner for our last night with them. She made a dinner of potato, carrot, hotdog, broth, onions and served it over rice with fresh pineapple. Not your everyday meal but we made it work.

A showed us how to operate the waste to biogas system he jury-rigged. His system is this: there is a five-gallon bucket in the shed. You use it for a toilet. Every few days, either Michael or I, haul that to the biogas deal and pour it in. This is the most revolting part of the whole operation but must be done. We now know what we need to know, along with a few tidbits like when it is termite season, put poison on the legs of the house to keep them down.

With the porch surrounding the house having screens half way up, everything that is outside is inside. And the ants, well, they hiked up two stories into the porch-kitchen. The termites and ants, little as they were, were overtaking things. Next, though, R mentioned that we should never stick our hands in dark corners, but if we do and we get bit by a scorpion, they won't kill you; it just numbs you a bit. Uh-huh!

Well, here's how that unfolded. One day a hummingbird flew into the kitchen and up toward the top of one wall. As I followed it, with my eyes, I saw a black scorpion that was about five times larger than any scorpion I ever saw and black. Once that hummer clued me in, I was on the lookout for them everywhere and they were everywhere. I found them behind the curtains, under the cloth that covered the generator, on the ceiling, and here is the god-awful truth. Miles tried to crush one with the head of a mop and it scrambled up the wall, across the ceiling, through a hole in the ceiling, near our bed and out, over the roof and dropped down, two stories, basically, into the moat surrounding the house, and then it swam away. That is 100% truth. That was the dealbreaker for me. From that day forward, I was ready to bolt.

Our second-to-last day with Y and R was easy. Y took me on a walkthrough of her plants and then we played scrabble with her. Later, we made Pina Coladas with pineapple squash (concentrated pineapple juice), powdered coconut cream (with hot water), and rum. Very tasty indeed! We played Scrabble again with Y and R in the evening.

The following morning, we chatted over coffee and did yoga together. We walked to Columbia, a 45-minute walk, one way, did email at the school, and gabbed with Denys, then went back to the farm and mowed a bit and gathered coconuts with R. We made more Pina Coladas and played more Scrabble. Y and R left for Belmopan and on to Hawaii.

Our first day alone, Miles and I got into a big fight and he moved to the guest room. I think that fight was long overdue, and this wasn't the most cohesive situation to be in with a rocky relationship, anyway. Then I spotted a big old tarantula sitting perfectly still near where I pee in the morning in the grass. Since everything is done outside, I became comfortable just walking down the steps and squatting right off the path. I hoped that I didn't get so used to this that I did it back in the States.

After a few days, Miles decided he didn't like sleeping alone in the guest room, so he moved back to the 'master.' It makes me laugh now thinking about it being the master bedroom. Nothing about it lent that name to it.

We both chopped our hair shorter and Miles shaved his mustache. The humidity was over the top and anything we could do to cool down was a plus. It was so humid that the metal on my bra straps rusted in the first two weeks I was there.

Eating all the fruit as it ripens became quite a challenge. A dozen bananas ripen all at once and after a while, they gagged me, so I started slicing and freezing them, which made them far more appealing. The papayas grew so big they were the size of watermelons, so once I ate one, I couldn't face another. Mangoes were so bountiful that I tried making mango pancakes, which were a huge success. Pineapples ripen three at a time and that is way beyond our ability to consume. Learning how to use these fruits and save them was a handful for me but I learned. Freezing was my go-to method. But our freezer was no bigger than a small mailbox. That limited the freezing capers.

We discovered a little eatery in a house near the sea in PG. Gomer, the owner, made us a lunch of tofu covered in a warm curry/turmeric sauce with vegetable rice and salad. It was spectacular. He cooked in the kitchen on his stove while we sat right near him at a small table. It was fun to see how he was making things work and it was interesting to get to know the guy. He was the spiritual type who, when he saw Miles suffering one day, from spraying too much DEET on himself to keep off bugs, felt his pain and told him, "Miles, you must soak in the sea, the salt water will heal you, that is what my mother taught me."

Gomer gave himself that name for his American self. He comes from San Lucia (West Indies) and that is the name of a tree that is used to make dugouts (canoes) and lasts forever. His real name is Ignatio.

The DEET incident was important to understand. Miles was very diligent at spraying his legs and arms every day. When we did garbage run, he carried the garbage and I followed him spraying his backside constantly to protect his skin from biting bugs. We brought with us the most powerful bug spray available with a large quantity of DEET, known to be effective at warding off bugs. Because he was so fastidious at it, he got seriously ill. He vomited, got cold sweats, and was very sick and weak, and at times was convulsive. I looked at our options. The yard was flooded a long way before the car which was now almost at the road due to all that rain. I would have to drag or carry him. All I could do was sit with him as he laid on the bed. I watched him convulse and suffer until he finally seemed to move through the worst of it. I never left his side but was basically helpless to know what to do. It didn't occur to us until later that he had poisoned himself with that spray. It didn't happen to me because I never remembered to use the spray, and because of that, every night I spent about an hour scratching my legs from the bites I got that day. Between being so hot and humid, and having that one hour of scratching and then the fear of scorpions crawling overhead, sleep for me was agonizing.

Since this farm was off the grid, there was no AC or fan or electricity, or phones in the house. The stove and fridge ran off of propane.

We hiked to Lubaantun after Miles got his strength back and asked the docent, Sango to give us a guided tour of the ruins. He shared stories he knew from his grandfather and his knowledge of the ruins that were built between 730 A.D. and 900 A.D., and he said that sometimes at night, he heard laughter in the courtyard. Getting to know him was a beautiful thing because he was trusting us with his true stories.

It rained so much that I began to collect water for entertainment. And because R offered me the opportunity to use his cache of paints in his little shed under the house and a basket of dried flowers the size of a fist, I began to paint murals. I did one entire wall over the stairway in the kitchen, floor to ceiling, wall to wall, attaching those dried flowers to branches of an enormous tree I drew with a tire swing hanging from one branch. Then I painted a mural on the porch of another tree with a tire swing hanging from a branch (this had become my personal logo, it gave me comfort) and painted all the kitchen cabinets white, and painted the steps up to the kitchen. It was my way of avoiding losing my mind with the 'Groundhog Day' feel of this life and all the critters that made life uncomfortable. I ended up writing a lengthy pain-filled poem about jungle life called; The Jungle and Me, Oxymorons, You See. That is when I came to understand how some of the greatest art is created through pain or from pain.

Miles went into his cave and though he did one mural on a porch wall, his normal go-to behavior that I'd seen over the time we were together was to go into seclusion. It looked like depression to me but I let him do what he had to do without trying to drag him out of it. So, painting everything in sight and collecting water kept me from going nuts. I painted four murals there, eventually.

The termites were making a path up the legs of the house, time to poison them, per R's instructions to keep the population from taking over. That night the frogs croaked deafeningly, one of the dogs got fired up, a radio played in the distance, and bugs were biting Miles, all at 1 a.m. Groan. It was a full moon. One frog found its way into our bedroom for god's sake!!! Now it's my turn to do poop patrol. Geeze! Gotta love living in the jungle. And now ants are marching up the legs of the house, two stories, straight into the kitchen and into the spices and oils. The jungle always wins.

If it doesn't rain every day, it rains several times a day. The yard is squishy and my car is now nearly at the road.

We found another newly discovered ruin, Uxbenka (oosh been ka) near San Antonio and Santa Cruz, where archaeologists are working on it in its early stage of discovery. We were lucky to find it empty and unprotected so that we could actually see how a ruin is found initially. We could see partly uncovered buried tombs, a temple crumbled with trees growing out of it, stelae laying on the ground with etchings in them, a small tent, and roofs over current dig sites. We climbed to the top of the highest pile of rubble, probably a temple, and saw sunken parts, one looked like a cave or entrance. It was so cool to find this ruin in its earliest stages of discovery. We learned so much from it and felt lucky to be there alone.

On our way back, we discovered a store in a house by spotting a Coca Cola sign on the siding near the door. We bought Cokes and were given permission to take pics of the kids peeking at us from behind the counter, and a woman processing Masa (corn) with a motorized contraption run with a huge belt. Another luck find today. Further down the road, I spotted three young boys, 11-years-old down to eight-years-old, walking with bundles of logs strapped together and strapped over their foreheads, and hanging down their backs, walking home. I said I was going to offer them a ride. Miles said no but I did anyway. I pulled over and asked them if they wanted a ride.

"Oh yes," they all yelled.

I opened the trunk and let them put their bundles inside and then they hopped in the back seat. When they pointed to their house, I stopped, opened the trunk, and tried to hand a bundle to one of the boys but I couldn't lift it! These little guys not only chopped this wood with machetes but were hauling it with ease.

Observations I made of myself while living in the jungle:

- I want long-suffering to be a 'thing' of the past.
- I know when my spirit is sinking, when the place isn't conducive to happiness for me.
- I don't like jungles, scorpions, and all that's included.
- I need communications with family on a regular basis.
- I need to 'be there,' to see for myself, whether I will like a place, a people, the climate.
- I have a need to see and feel new places.
- I've noticed that certain women—solid and grounded women, are drawn to me, and I am greatly blessed by this.
- I've come to trust my intuition.
- I love animals.
- I hate feeling 'sticky' and intense sweating.
- I can cope for periods with poor weather, poor tools, poor conditions, poor equipment and see the humor in it—for a while. There is a limit!!!
- I've lost all vanity. With the primitive living situation here, there is no room for it. We shower outside in the wide open. I can't stand much clothing on, sweat washes away any lotion or make-up, my hair is either wet from a shower or wet from sweat.

- I believe one purpose for me, in being here, is for the dogs. I feel torn. I want to set them free. I hate seeing them tied to short chains with no life, no human love, and no freedom. My dream is to set them free. I hate seeing their destitute lives and not being able to help them.

Miles emailed Y and R to let them know we wanted to leave early. Y said she would make it happen but then realized she made commitments that kept them away into August. That was anguishing to learn. But a quote I found of Shirley MacLaine's speaks to me:

"We are not victims of the world we see; we are victims of the way we see the world." From her book Dancing in the Light.

We went to Lubaantun to have a ceremony. We took incense, a lighter, our Mayan whistles, paper and pens, and meditated first. Then, after sitting with the energy of the site, we wrote down things we wished to remove from our lives and things we wished to bring into our lives. We burned them in the altar and meditated again. Now I'm trying to figure out a way to make this jungle stay less depressing and more positive. I thought about water production, then about selling Jungle Recipes, I couldn't come up with much.

A few recipes I did learn to like and make are:

Jungle Papaya Chicken:

- 3 Tsp. turmeric
- 1 large (watermelon size) or 3 small green (unripe) papayas
- 4 cloves fresh garlic, diced
- ½ white onion, diced
- Olive oil
- 1 whole free-range chicken-cut up
- ½ green pepper, diced
- 3 sticks celery, diced
- 1 large carrot, chopped
- Salt and pepper

Peel and cut in half papaya. Remove seeds and chop into chunks. Chop carrot into chunks. Sauté, briefly in olive oil and add 1 cup of water and simmer till fork tender. In another frying pan, sauté onion, garlic, green pepper and celery. Set aside. Sauté chicken parts in oil on both sides, add ½ cup water and simmer till tender, 30 minutes. Mash papaya/carrot mixture and add turmeric, Salt and pepper. Mix with onion mixture and add to chicken pot. Simmer together 15 – 20 minutes or until flavors blend.

Serve with Basmati rice:

Put 2 cups water and 1 cup rice in pot, blend together and bring to a boil with ½ Tbsp. cumin, 1 tsp turmeric, ½ tsp salt and 14 tsp pepper. Turn off heat and let sit 15 – 20 minutes.

Black Bean/Salsa/Mac and Cheese Gumbo

Cook 1 cup dried black beans 1-1 ½ hours or until tender.

<u>Make Salsa:</u>

- 1 small can of diced tomatoes
- ½ onion diced
- 4 cloves garlic

Sauté onion and garlic and add tomatoes. Cook together for ½ hour. Prepare mac and cheese according to package instructions (today, avoiding packaged foods, I make everything from scratch, fresh.) So, mac and cheese is simple: cook the mac, melt a chunk of real cheddar or other cheese you love in a pan with milk or cream and butter. The proportions are according to your taste. Blend the sauce thoroughly and pour over the drained mac. Add ¼ cup salsa to cooked beans and simmer 10 minutes.

Layer mac and cheese, beans, salsa and serve hot.

Very delicious.

We've been in the jungle for 45 days and it rained 40.5 inches. I washed clothes, it rained on the clothes; I re-wrung them out and hung them again, it rained on them again. Then it rained a third time. Storm # 4 is threatening at the moment. The moat is now loudly flowing around the house and toward Cacao Creek. I had to work at finding the positivity in it. I thought, *Well, those clothes have been rinsed over and over so they should be really clean and fresh now!*

We heard from Y and R. They will be able to come home early to release us and said they will never do this to caretakers again. We were the seventh and they see that we've all had a miserable existence here.

My car developed a problem and the locals helped us out by getting us connected to two guys who knew cars. A cable broke. They worked on it and charged next to nothing for it, $40 Belize. It isn't too hard to imagine how a cable would break here. Very bad roads and a lot of dust as well as constant rain. If this rain and humidity rusted the metal on my bra straps, why not!!! The rains come; the rains go, seven times as of 8:15, the morning of July 3. We have been here 48 days. We left when another black scorpion showed up in our bedroom. That was the final deal breaker. It was a day earlier than Y wanted us to leave but we'd had it.

On our way out of town, everything looked a whole lot brighter to us. The skies were blue and the sun shone brightly. The air smelled fresh and the homes and shops all looked way better now. A change of perspective. Gratitude is the word. We stayed at the D Victoria just like we did on entering Belize. The sun is still shining. No rain. We were at the border crossing early the next morning and Miles was apprehensive, but the guards didn't care about us leaving. It was entering that they cared about. If we got in, they would let us out. I was the driver. Next, we found a hotel in Villahermosa that turned out to be a secret rendezvous place where everything is glued or nailed down and a curtain covered our car in the garage. Been there, done that.

The next day we ended up in another Hotel de Eros. Curtains cover our car again. This time in Poza Rica. Hmmm. On our way out of this town, the roads looked like they were bombed out. At one point I watched a car go down the road ahead of me and just disappear. I was alarmed wondering what just happened and approached slowly to examine how that unfolded. Some roads caved off the sides, some entire roads caved in. That slowed things down a whole lot and the topes were enough to tear the bottom off a car.

This time we crossed over into the states at Brownsville, TX. And I couldn't have been happier. The total mileage on my car was 7585.5 miles. From May 1 – July 10, we put those miles on. My car was never the same. I wasn't either.

Tootie

How loving Tootie through the autumn of her years pushed all of our buttons all the time. And it helped us evolve into a more caring, loving family. It was almost impossible at first to get past that drama that our family had learned as coping mechanisms. But in time we did, to some degree. I'm not gonna lie, there were times when her unrest or agitation over something drew out her feisty side and she would tweak our hard-won good natures. Of course, there were always days when she was feeling powerless or worse, useless, causing her to put us to the ultimate test of patience. She felt the loss of control that she once had. Because she was an extremely active, 'hands-on' woman, losing her strength and memory crushed her every day of those years when she lived with her oldest daughter, Sybil.

Peyton, Todd (now deceased), and I were on and off participants in her care and added interest to her life. By passing the baton now and then, any one of us did not get too burned out or frustrated to such a degree that we found it hard to be kind and patient. And something that I found notable was that when one of us was losing it, another would jump in and help that one back away before they lost it. Everyone needed a break from this very important, yet sometimes formidable, role. None of us, ever, wanted Tootie to be placed in a nursing facility. We had seen what happens to people who are and Tootie actually worked at a nursing home, so she really knew the inside workings of a home and what happened to those left there. I know that for some it is the only option but for us it was never an option. And I can say with complete pride that every difficult moment just made us better people and without having her right in the middle of our lives, we would have missed some very important moments. I like the fact that 'hard' doesn't mean impossible, and 'trying' doesn't mean we can't get through it. I will always be so proud of us for doing our best at keeping Tootie safe and warm, and right in the middle of all of our lives.

I like to view life challenges like this as opportunities to see who I am and to dig down deep in order to understand who Tootie is and was. To know her and her unresolved issues (which always manifest in later years) was to help us understand what made her tick. It was good for me to learn to love her even when I felt so frustrated with her and to always remember what so many people told me that she did the best she knew how to do.

When I look back now to a time when she was 87 and still so viable and so mentally sound, and without question, jumped right into the fray to help us take care of her youngest son, Todd, through his last days, I am so proud of her. I love knowing that at that age, she fearlessly dove right in to give what she had to him every day. It makes me proud to know the pain she carried in her heart and yet she stayed right with the program.

Tootie did not know how to show her love or how to nurture. I assume that it is because she did not feel loved and nurtured, and thus did not know how to be so. She was, in my eyes, a mother who was never mothered, so she didn't know how to give what she never got. I admit to craving her love and nurturing most of my life and it was only recently that I came to understand that she really didn't have it in her.

Today, at the age of almost 95, she is still pretty and still cares about how she looks. She still wants her hair done weekly and still takes care of her fingernails. Looking at how she wears her watch, I gather that she was lefthanded and was forced to be righthanded. Back in her day kids were punished for not being righthanded. She wears her watch on her right hand just like someone would who is lefthanded. Maybe if I knew more about the life Tootie had as a little girl, I would be crushed and deeply saddened. But I would also have even more empathy for her.

For me, Tootie was someone I always craved to know and understand. And I craved her love. Getting inquisitive with her just created angst in her and she would usually throw me an answer that was no answer at all. For instance, I would ask her, 'Mom, what was Christmas like when you were a kid?'

Her answer, 'We were poor.'

Longing to know her just made her go underground. When she was very young, and as the first live birth of her parents, she was given away to her aunt to raise. I don't think she ever really knew why this happened. Kids then were told nothing. I could only summarize through talking with friends and other family members that her aunt and uncle had no children, so she was given to them. Other thoughts were that maybe her mom and dad could not afford to feed all of their kids. They had seven kids, total.

I realize that the above lingo is not necessarily politically correct but then neither is much else in this book. It is bare bones truth. Raw truth. No sugar coating. On good days you will read good and loving words. On crazy-making days you will read exactly what was felt and said. How better to walk in our moccasins through a very trying and yet enriching time in our lives.

From the point when we lost Todd, who was a mere 52 years of age, seven years ago, up until about three years ago, Tootie was very capable and quick on her feet. She prided herself, in fact, on how well her mind worked. She saw herself as a ring leader of sorts, one who delegated and supervised projects. Nothing thrilled her more than to kibitz on how something is being done and how she thinks there is always a better way. And her eyes are constantly scanning the horizon looking for things that need fixing or should be cut down or cleaned up or built. She feels like a master-mind at deciphering what needs to be done which always includes delegating, key word here!

That habit is so ingrained in her that we can't break her of it. She still wants to mother us by 'reminding' us to tie our shoes, so to speak and to eat enough. In her era, a woman was a mother and after the kids left home, 'if she let them,' her purpose was done. The empty nest era referred to her era and those before her. Not so today. We women, today, know what to do when the childrearing days are over. We set fire to a new plan and a new us!

Her idea of a fun day was gardening, pickling, canning, laundry, staining the shingles on the house, raking the yard, and so on. Work was her passion. Maybe considering that there was never extra money for fun times, that is all that she could afford to do for entertainment. She never drank or smoked. Imagine living that cleanly!!!

When I was a young child, in the spring, (commonly called spring cleaning by Tootie), we took the mattresses off our beds and put them out in the yard along with the bed frames and springs (box springs were not invented yet), and beat the mattresses and hosed down the frames and springs. Then we washed all walls and ceilings in the house and all windows. Either she was a clean freak or the coal furnace that heated our home polluted the heck out of it!

Years later, long after the coal furnace was replaced and even beyond moving out of that old homestead, we were still washing walls and ceilings. Only now we were in a home, Tootie and Homer built by hand from scratch. The tradition remained for long years after moving into our new, more modern home with a gas furnace.

Ironing clothes, washing walls, and ceilings were never going to be a part of my life. I put that notion in the delete file before I even imagined getting married and having kids. And I knew from the get-go that I would never, ever be Mrs. so and so. I would always be Rona. No extensions of someone else were acceptable. I was going to be my own person. Sybil designed her life the same way. I never saw her in a freshly ironed shirt. If it was wrinkled, it just needed another toss in the dryer.

I saw way too clearly what little gratification women got, let alone applause from all the work they did as wives and mothers. They were not valued or appreciated by the majority of society and men in particular. I know! I was there! I saw it and felt it.

Even as a wee child, I was asking Tootie why she didn't ask more of my father. He could come home from work and fall asleep in the chair right after dinner. She said that he worked all week and brought home a paycheck, and that was enough. Expectations speak volumes! It is as simple as this…go back to the generations before my parents' time, back to the mid-1800s. Life was even harder and yet because people didn't know any difference and had nothing to compare, they just dealt with the status quo. If a person was able to find the little nuggets of gold buried in each day's work, they could find joy and happiness and a feeling of satisfaction.

I'll bet if my kids look back on my life years from now, they will scratch their heads in wonderment, too. They know me intimately. I have shared my truths, my story, my past, and my pain. They know me. And yet, they will wonder. Each one of them is different in their amazingness and I know them. Or at least I know a lot about them. And my grandkids. Oh, my goodness! What will they think about how I did things and how I lived? My grandkids teethed on computers, DVDs, etc.

One thing can be said for me, I don't quit on people. I turn myself inside out to try to make relationships work. Eventually, though, I will quit. When my spirit dies for someone, it is over. And I never know when that final straw will break. I never know when I will walk away for good but I will; that is for certain.

So, we are what we are in spite of and because of our parents. They write on our wall early on. From birth, until we leave home, they write on our wall. The wall of our psyche. And that wall is what we go to for answers and responses to life's dilemmas. Until that is, we discover that we have an 'eraser' and can remove all that has been written, and begin to write our own truths on that wall. For example, your father will display how to handle stress and you as a small child will absorb that information, and it will go straight to and become etched on 'your wall.' Your mother will inform you by way of her behavior, how to handle arguments and how to love. Her information will also get etched directly on your wall. And you will go back to that freaking wall all of your life for directions as to how to handle life's issues!!! I'm serious! Watch out for what's on that wall!

We ultimately create who we are and what we will become. We design and create our destiny. No one but us. That is how much power we have. We shape, mold, chisel, nudge, examine, and manifest what it is we see as our purpose. And purposes change! For example, there is the time of mothering followed by the time of menopausal change which leads to the caterpillar becoming the butterfly. The best kept secret is that menopause is a gift. It cracks open the core of who we are and kicks to the curb that which we are not. The closet gets cleaned out and our world excludes the people who do not value us or serve our highest good.

During Tootie's era menopause was seen as a curse. But then so was a woman's moon cycle. Menopause was said to make a woman crazy. The crazy that does show up is a good crazy. It peels off the wraps of the façade. All that is not and never was the real deal. No more nice girl! Now it is time for the powerful one to stand up. The Wonder Woman who has been hiding beneath her 'nice girl' façade.

Tootie, sadly, never got to experience Wonder Woman. She has always been in victim mode.

Hence the saying, "if you think you are not smart, then you aren't, if you think you are not important, then you aren't."

Our mother, at 94, is locked like cement in her ways. She is too far along on her journey and does not want to be nudged out of her mold and comfort zone. Just a bit of advice for future sandwich people, pay close attention to how your mother and father are beneath all their layers. Because you will be living with all that as well as all their unresolved issues down the road, one way or another.

Here is a synopsis of a day in the life of Tootie. She gets up all chirpy, pours a cup of her favorite joe loaded with cream and a good 5 – 6 tablespoons of sugar. If the coffee is strong enough for a spoon to stand up in it, all is well. Two pieces of potato bread toast, lathered with butter is breakfast. If you even think about sitting down with her and asking how she is, you have just derailed your morning. Because she will tell you exactly how she slept, how many times she got up to pee, and then goes straight to all the bad news she read in last night's paper. Her mind magnetizes to all bad news and nothing thrills her more than to regurgitate it to innocent bystanders.

After breakfast, she dives into a fierce game of solitaire. She may play for hours. If you happen to sit down anywhere within ear shot after she got her monthly bank statement, you might as well just go ahead and shoot yourself. Finances have become a raging topic with her. Here's the irony, she will have just flown to Wisconsin for a couple weeks' visit and when the bill shows up on her credit card statement or bank statement, she rages. She demands to know why someone is taking out several airline tickets off of her account when she has not flown. She said she drove to Wisconsin. In her mind, Wisconsin is now neighboring Arizona and just a short ride away.

She took me off of her former bank account as POA because automatic withdrawals were happening every month, and she did not order anything. Two dozen magazines showed up as well as a large supply of wrinkle cream and she knows she didn't order any of it. Thus, I must have ordered those items. Her short-term memory 90% of the time is fleeting unless you are whispering something that you don't want her to hear. Then the facts will get embedded in her memory to be thrown out every 30 seconds throughout the day.

Finding herself living to the ripe old age of 94 befuddles her and causes serious anguish. Everything is hard. Getting up is hard, sitting down is hard, walking is hard, carrying anything is hard, dressing is hard, putting on socks and shoes is hard, remembering is hard, showering is hard, and living with three of her kids is hard. If she could move in with one of her brothers or her Wisconsin son, she believes life would be good. Living in Arizona doesn't float her boat. She wants to look out the window and see what she saw in the last 90 years. Her old garden, the flowers she planted eons ago, the maple trees, the swing, the school yard adjacent to the house, and the old golf course across the way. And she wants to be able to drive to her hair salon, card games at the Legion, and to church. Sadly, driving privileges had to be taken away.

She doesn't remember this but I do. When we took away Homer's driving privileges as well as his beloved truck, he confiscated the riding lawnmower and used it to get around. He rode it up and down the neighborhood mowing one strip across everyone's yard. He mowed the garden slicing the squash up, he drove it to the golf course and into the creek, stopping only when a large boulder jammed under the axle. Tootie put tires around all her fruit trees so that they didn't get mowed down. He was happy-go-lucky because he found another way to get around. He opened up a five-quart pail of ice cream and grabbed a spoon. What's not to like about this? The way he meandered through his final years was with an ever-present childlike joy. Tootie, on the other hand, is cranked up most of the time. She is a Gemini. One of her twins is the sweet church lady. The other is the evil, sneaky one. If you think this is funny or mean, you have not walked a mile in my moccasins or even slipped them on for a glimpse of what life is like here. In the interest of looking at the humorous side of this adventure, I am bearing the raw truth. No better way to learn and grow than to walk through it.

Hearing aids. This is one issue that is a quandary for Tootie's hearing people. A simple comment made to her in lightness can turn violent in a nanosecond after a series of 'huhs.' After repeating a remark multiple times, it is guaranteed to raise hackles on the one wishing to share something so simple with her. I think twice before making simple remarks weighing how many times I will have to reiterate and how much the value will be lost.

Peyton, Sybil, and I are very active and love to be doing many things each day. On a normal day, I might do laundry, hang my clothes on the clothesline to dry, work in the garden, cook dinner, hike up the trail, and clean up the kitchen. Tootie resents not being able to do all that too. She hates that she can't do all that she once did. Her daily mantra is this: I am useless, I am old and rickety, I am no help, your day is coming, and so on. No amount of reinforcement of her values and contributions sinks in. She wants to see herself in that light. She wants to continue feeling useless.

We take turns getting her to her hairdresser, purchasing her favorite daily items such as cream, butter, potato bread, and coffee, as well as playing Hand and Foot or Scrabble with her. All three of us make time every day to do this game playing with her. And we all ask for her assistance preparing dinner.

What I am seeing is that who she is and who she was as a young mother is one in the same. I just didn't see it growing up. Now I do. I see things so clear it awes me. What I felt and saw growing up is just way more pronounced today. As a young mother she never wanted to listen. She was always thinking of what she wanted to say while someone was sharing something with her. She does that today. She resented a show of pure delight and excitement and would try to squash it. She does that today if given the chance. I don't give her the chance. She always felt overworked even though she loved to keep busy. She makes us aware of how much she has worked by moaning and groaning under her breath, and the timing is always right when we are in the room; same behavior, different age.

One day I was trying to rest up for my night shift job and found that she was tracking me no matter where I went. I saw her need and asked her if she wanted to play a game of Scrabble out on the deck. She lit right up. Later, I am down on the patio in another part of the house and she tracked me down again. I looked at her anguished face and said to myself, *why does Tootie have separation anxiety?* The realization came to me. As a young teen, she was sent to live with her aunt and uncle who lived an hour's drive away from her home. She was the oldest child and a daughter which made no sense to me. But being able to go there in my heart, I can see why she feels lonely in her own skin. She feels abandoned if no one is sharing her space with her. She gets really pissed if she gets up and can't locate every one of us.

She will say, "No one even thought to leave me a note, so I just went back to bed!"

She is seething with anger and resentment. Unresolved issues lay dormant in our psyches but they don't go away ever. If not addressed, they will pop up later in life.

Tootie's inability to love and nurture her kids likely came from being raised without those human needs. She gave what she got. Just a guess but it sure makes sense. Her secrets were locked securely inside her so guessing is my only means to the end.

What I have done to protect myself and still be able to love and nurture her is to examine, safeguard, and shield myself from those old behaviors, so that she can continue to be who she is (and there is no other way at this point) and I don't allow her behavior to hurt me or diminish me.

One thing I have discovered is that outsiders fall in love with Tootie quickly because they only see her church lady side—the one she wisely projects to the outside world. And no one, bar none, can even begin to think they know the Tootie that we know. That is why I believe that some kids abandon their parents in old age. It seldom is the kids being bad people. They are giving back what they got.

I try hard not to do this with her but if I am honest, I have to admit that sometimes those old feelings of resentment are still lingering inside my heart and mind, and I give her a little of what she gave me. I am the lucky one to have been born in an era when people know to examine themselves and to walk the high road. Because we are fortunate to have three of us caring for Tootie; we can nudge each other when we are losing it with her or to give each other a break when time away is needed.

Everyone is quick to offer advice to us about how to care for our 'wonderful' Tootie. Sybil and I were commiserating about it recently. She said that if she shares a typical day with a girlfriend that friend will unequivocally throw out this comment, "Oh I lost my mother five years ago and I miss her every day!"

My sister says their comments always make her feel guilty. A friend of mine shares her trials living with her 94-year-old mother and then reads an article in the newspaper about how to care for elders and how to understand where they are coming from. The article is summed up with these words, "Be patient and understand that they are living in their past because their present short-term memory is fleeting or gone. You would want the same for you, wouldn't you?"

Another guilt trip. My friend, Mela, gets teary when she shares this article with me and for the rest of the night, I think about how I could do better. I resolve to be more loving, and kind, and I'll be damned if the minute Tootie and I meet up the next morning, she doesn't get me cranked up with some mood she has settled into. She starts off the morning bemoaning how no one is ever there to talk to and so there is no point in wearing her hearing aids.

No good deed goes unpunished. Sitting down with her wanting to improve my treatment of her, she quickly dashes away any hope by pushing multiple buttons all at once in just a moment's time. Only she can do this to me and my siblings. She has the power to raise our hackles in a microsecond.

Here is a button that she has always pushed with me. I always strived to be her protector and to do a lot for her to make her life happier. Because I witnessed so much meanness directed toward her emanating from Homer in his drunken stupors, I appointed myself her protector because she played the victim role and was so attached to that role that nothing and nobody was going to shake her out of it. I tried!!! Countless times when I confronted Homer, she cringed and shrunk back in fear and looked at me, rather than him, as the problem. She thought I had a lot of power and she didn't like it.

When I did favors or kindnesses for her, every time, she would say to me, "Someone did this or that for me." I say, (in times of being ungrounded), "Oh, you forgot my name now and my name is 'someone'?"

It was and is her way of not acknowledging and giving credit for good deeds. It is a part of a game she feels the need to play. It has been a lifelong thing with her. The achievers in our family, the strong ones, got kicked to the curb and the weak, failing, struggling, ne'er-do-wells always get all the kudos and praise. It is another of her games. I can look at it today and say that is how she feels inside herself. She feels like a failure. She was a mother before she turned 17, had been married since 16, baby was on the way before she got married, been a mother for 78 years. WOW!

Back in her day, there was a lot more shame attached to having a baby out of wedlock. Not so today. Today, in my view, getting married without a lot of forethought is a step that is almost certain to pack a ton of regret and future divorce within its realm. Anyway, for Tootie back then, it was likely a situation that brought a lot of angst with it. And who knows the shame and blame that got wrapped inside that predicament. To mask Tootie's regrets and feelings of hopelessness, she took on the victim role. That way everything looked to her like it was outside her realm of responsibility.

Nothing makes a child of a victim/mother more enraged and warriorlike than years of observation of this behavior. I remember, as a young lady, wondering why she kept crying every time Homer fought with her rather than rage and go after his throat. Crying after decades of this drama seemed like a losing proposition to me. As a result of watching her do this all my life, I turned into a physical warrioress. When someone wronged me, and after talking didn't work, I went for the throat. All my rage is mine and hers combined. It is mine because I invited situations and relationships into my life that came packaged with all the lessons I needed in order to peel away buried resentment and pain from growing up in a dysfunctional home. When I chose someone who was controlling, didn't listen, flirted with other women in front of me, directed their meanness at me, my hands were tied, and I was stymied for the longest time! It took beginning to become conscious and awaken to my inner journey as well as dredging up old wounds and making sense of them before letting them go. I invited all of these behaviors into my life and suffered immensely before looking at my actions and these men to see what a gift they brought to my life. They were mere teachers and I was getting the lessons! That is the gift that all this is about. Peeling away the layers of old stuff, old pain and suffering, old feelings of not being loved or even liked, not being valued, not being seen, releases all that buried pain and the behaviors that were attached to each. Now I can look at Tootie and draw a shield around my heart and place her in a part of my world where she has no power over my heart or feelings or thinking. And I can be good and kind to her, take care of her and protect her without giving her any power to hurt me any longer. I don't have to know the whys of how she came to be who she is. I just have to know who I want to be and who I came here to be.

Every one of us has value beyond our understanding. We all came here to discover who we are at our core, what our strengths and passions and purpose are and go after it with intensity. When we are on fire about our lives, we know we have uncovered why we are here.

We are born into situations but we are not of them. We are born into families and so often we don't fit. We don't feel like we belong. It is because we came to serve our highest good and the family we are born into, often serves up the best lessons on how to realize the pearl that we are. They are the sand that creates our pearl.

Peyton, Sybil, and I invested in keeping Tootie out of a nursing home and keeping her amongst family where she is loved and cared for. She doesn't value or appreciate her life with us. She wants to be where she is not. We puzzle over what to do with this situation. How to open her up to the good fortune that she lives with is our dilemma. At her age, she could be sitting with her peers in a home somewhere and everyone around her would be drooling, staring off in space with minds that long ago checked out, or sleeping in their wheel chairs. Instead she lives with constant challenges, inspiration, adventure, conversation, activities, great meals shared, and is rarely alone. What's not to like about that! I know as well as I know my own name that we are all in this drama for reasons that are out of our understanding at the moment. Just as caring for Todd till he died provided soul growth so does this situation.

I hope that by sharing the nuts and bolts of how life really is with Tootie in her 'golden' years, I can give you— the reader—permission to get in touch with your rage and your childhood wounds, and work through it all while seeing this opportunity as a gift and a blessing. Life is all about growth; heart and soul growth as well as enlightenment. We all have so much more to learn and give if we open up to it. There is not a single one of us here on this earth that has reached their full potential. Only by opening up to the unknown, uncertainty, and moving outside our comfort zones, can we stretch and grow to our fullest extent.

An excerpt from a typical morning conversation.

Tootie: "How are you?"

Me: "Good, how are you?"

T: "Oh, old and rickety"

M: Silence

T: "I got up several times last night to pee."

M: Silence

This morning had more meat in it.

Tootie: Frantically filling the sink with soap and hot water and dishes. The suds becoming mountainous in her frenzy.

T: "Sybil left."

M: "Oh!"

T: "She left without saying a word!"

M: "Oh"

T: "I was sitting right there and she didn't say a word!!!"

M: "Oh"

T: "I'm just worried something is wrong with Joe!" (Joe is Sybil's partner)

M: Silence

T: Frantically moving dishes around the sink, "Do you have some time today to take me to the bank?"

M: "No, I just got home from work at 3:30 a.m. I need to rest today."

T: "Well, I need to go to the bank!"

M: Silence

T: "You sure you can't take me to the bank?"

M: "No mom, I need to rest today."

T: "Well, I can't bike there! I haven't got a nickel."

M: "Breathe, don't take on her stuff!!!"

T: "I took an envelope to the bank a month ago and need to go get it."

M: Silence, thinking, *don't feed into her frenzy. Don't get yourself wrapped around the axle with her.*

That is how my mother likes to fill her life with drama. I like to start the day easy, with coffee, silent, staring off into space, thinking my thoughts, feeling happy to feel good.

She has always needed drama. As a child and young adult, I observed this but didn't really get it until now that this is who my mother is. If she can dive into a rabid discussion of all the bad things that she read in this morning's paper and basically dump all of it on me, it will be a good day for her. Why she seeks the negativity is a mystery to me. I won't even read the paper or listen to the news anymore in order to practice living in peace and to keep myself in balance and harmony.

The bottom line of this treasure trove of experience—caring for our elderly parent—is that there is unfathomable, untold, opportunity to grow, learn, overcome, and trust in the good that comes from 'doing the right thing.'

Homer, Coming Full-Circle

We gathered at the picture window facing the golf course and spotted Homer, looking frantically from the creek to the house, wringing his hands, his eyes darting back and forth in panic. What was in the creek? What had him so troubled? What was he doing there?

Peyton and Todd ran down to where he was standing and looked into the creek. Homer looked down there too. He was wondering what to do. No words were needed. They ran back to Peyton's truck; there was always a towrope in the back. They loved Homer and knew just what to do to help him. With the skills they had, they pulled that mower out without a word. Because Peyton and Todd were the last kids born, Homer raised them to be more like companions. They were used to the unexpected lately, too.

Homer slipped into a rather comforting never-never land that we didn't see coming. He wasn't really sure of much anymore once this confused state snagged most of his clarity, but he was always happy. As long as he had his wheels, his non-filtered Camels, his whiskey and his peppermint candies, life was good.

On the sly, one day, when no one was looking, he took a five-quart bucket of ice cream out of the freezer, grabbed a spoon, and sat down in his favorite chair at the table. A big toothless grin lit up his face. He had nixed his dentures years ago and gummed his food from then on. Of course, the inevitable happened. Tootie walked into the room and spotted him. She had to be stealth to whisk that bucket out of his clutches and replace it with a bowl. He just wasn't working with a full deck anymore. The only way to understand how it was for him was to hide and watch. For us it was humorous but not so much for Tootie. He was a real thorn in her side.

The morning when she got up to make her beloved morning coffee and found that Homer had beat her to the punch was a nasty way to start her day. He had put the water in where the grounds go and the grounds where the water goes. That gummed up the works, and instead of her smelling fresh coffee anytime soon, she was up to her elbows cleaning up the mess. I could almost hear her grit her teeth.

Once his truck was sold, after a hair-raising ride, and his keys were confiscated, he became sly at sneaking everyone else's keys and hiding them. He probably thought procuring keys was the first step to driving again Once he hid them, though, they were lost to him too. We all learned the hard way by having to play the game out and from then on remembered the rules of engagement in that house. After one hunt for keys no one ever forgot to keep them in their pockets.

One of my favorite memories is this; one sunny day, Homer drove the Ryder around the garden slicing up the squash and chopping off all the other crops. The fruit trees would have gone down the same road, too, had Tootie not placed tires around each one. She had worked hard to plant that garden and now it looked like a disaster but she had become desensitized to his capers by now.

Next, he took a ride up to our old neighborhood, just a block away, and gave every yard one good swipe before heading back home. He was a beauty, with his cigarette hanging from his lip, fishing hat tilted sideways on his head, guiding that mower carefully down every yard. His face lit up with pride as he returned home, feeling satisfied with his work. That mower was life itself to him. It got him where he wanted to go and provided a sense of purpose.

Because the old neighborhood was still the same, his style of mowing alarmed no one. It was an old neighborhood and yards were not manicured back then. The neighbors had been there as long as we had—for decades. They were more like family, knew each other's history and helped raise each other's kids.

Sundowner's Syndrome and the effects of dementia caused Homer to be confused about where home was. It was puzzling and sad to have him beg to go home with us after a visit.

Even though we said, "This is your home,"

He said, "Nope, it isn't."

The neighbors kept finding him in their houses. He was looking for home and only he knew what that 'home' looked like. That was heartbreaking to see.

Tootie moved him to the nursing home when he tried to drink a glass of gasoline. It looked like his beloved whiskey. On a visit there one day, I asked him, "Do you know who I am?"

"You know who you are," he said, as he pulled out a selection of pantyhose, caps, and socks from his pockets. The nurse, walking by just then commented, "We don't care about that, we all share."

He was surely a handful for them now and hopefully provided some humor to their days.

Running Out of Gas and the
Surprise Gifts That Showed Up

I was on my way across the country on a road trip from Arizona to Wisconsin and was driving my old '86 4Runner. My phone was playing music, Michael Bublé's Christmas songs, and it was December.

I love Bublé's music a lot and as I was moving through the states heading east, a trip I had done countless times, with the volume up high and singing along. I got so into the flow and the music that I got lost in it and forgot to pay attention to my gas gauge. As I drove up a steep hill in Oklahoma, I think, my car suddenly just died. I looked at the gauges and saw that the needle on the gas gauge was at empty. I rolled over onto the shoulder and thought a minute about where the heck I was and what to do. I knew nothing about where I was, that's how lost I was in the music. On some level I had to have known to stay on a particular highway but otherwise I had no clue.

I looked to my right and saw a slope down, steep but not too steep, into a small dip, and then back up to a frontage road. There was nothing in the way like fencing, trees, or rocks, so I turned the wheel and headed down, coasting in neutral, rolling slowly and back up the slight rise and with repeated lurches got myself up onto the frontage road. Having a stick shift was vital right now. I continued lurching a few steps at a time up a two-lane country road by popping the clutch until I found a farm on my right. I continued inching into the driveway, close to the house. I got out, walked up a few steps across the porch and knocked on the door.

A lot of things could have gone wrong with that plan (which was by the seat of your pants), no one came to the door. I hoped a woman would be home, not a man. I turned and walked toward the barn, figuring that all farms kept remnant gas cans tucked in corners here and there. As I approached the barn, I heard a voice,

"Hello, can I help you?"

I turned abruptly and looked at where the voice was coming from. A woman was standing there looking at me. Lucky for me I hadn't yet crossed the line of stealing gas.

I turned and walked back to the steps leading up to her. I said, "I just ran out of gas."

She looked at me in complete confusion.

"You just ran out of gas in my driveway?" she said.

"Nope, I ran out on the highway and inched my way to your driveway. Can you help me get gas for my car?"

"I'm going to let my dogs out and then go get dressed, and when I return, I'll take you in my car to get gas, you should get in your car and wait," she said.

She promptly let the dogs out, big farm dogs, and they wandered around the yard.

I sat there thinking about what a complete cluster I might be in if she didn't actually return and left those dogs out; I was not only stuck because of being out of gas but stuck because what if those dogs were mean.

Minutes ticked by and finally she popped out of the front door and called the dogs in. I breathed a huge sigh of relief. Then she signaled for me to climb into her van with her. I ran over and hopped in so relieved that I couldn't believe my luck. As she started up the van, she began to spill out to me all of her troubles, her sadness, and her life story. I had known her five minutes. Before we were out of her driveway, I heard more than I thought was possible.

She told me that she had given up a baby when she was a very young girl because she was too young to be a mom. The baby as a son and every year since then, at Christmas, she fell into depression worrying about how he is and if he's happy. She had asked her coworkers at the middle school where she cooked if they thought she should hunt for a way to contact her son. They said to leave it alone. She sunk deeper into depression and every single Christmas since she gave him up, some 20 years, she spent in depression.

Her husband was a trucker and was seldom home. She had gained a ton of weight likely because of her sad life and when I showed up, I broke her out of her darkness. She poured out all of her sadness to me just like that. Now she had a listening ear and someone who felt her pain.

I told her, without a doubt, that she must seek her son out. I knew several adopted kids and they never stopped wondering why they were given away. They always had a hole in their heart, wondering if they weren't good enough, and it seemed to keep them from leading fulfilling lives. I encouraged her to hunt for him.

She took me to a gas station which was also a quick mart and she went into the store to buy me a gas can. I said that I would buy it but she insisted on buying my can, my gas, snacks, and drinks for the road, and then when I hugged her and we agreed to stay in touch, she directed me how to get back onto the highway leading east.

I will always think of that experience as a rich opportunity to see how accidents and mistakes can lead to tremendous blessings. I was super lucky to find a woman home, or anyone home, a farm that close to where I needed it to be, and that my showing up in that moment was a pure blessing for her. She needed a woman to show up to hear her pain and support her need to hunt for her child. I had many other thoughts but didn't volunteer them.

First, a husband who is never home is not good; a trucker, well, I have my thoughts about that avenue of work, heard too many stories, looking at her weight, I knew she was going without in so many ways.

If I could go back to that moment right now, I would stay with her for the day and talk it out more, and get an idea if she was hearing me or not. I will always wonder if she acted on my advice. The thought of her continuing to live the way she was, entrenched in misery, felt wrong to my soul.

I emailed her when I got to Wisconsin but never heard from her. My email may have gone into spam or she didn't have the heart to answer me. I'll never know. I do know that I was meant to cross paths with her that day.

What Happens to You When You Vision Quest?

HERE'S MY STORY.

When my life felt like it was up for grabs and I was living in the midst of chaos while renting a room at Sybil's ranch, in Hartford, New Mexico where the presence of newcomers, conflict, and drama was a constant, I went to my room and decided it was time for a change. I hunkered down in my bed and pondered what to do to create that change, and what I wanted it to look like.

Through an online search, I found a Vision Quest offered by a man named Hawk. His company, Quests by Hawk, out of Las Cruces, New Mexico held Quests all over the country. One that appealed to me was held in the Aldo Leopold Wilderness in New Mexico. I liked it because it was within driving distance, looked doable and was fairly inexpensive. I wasn't in great physical condition but also wasn't completely out of shape either because I hiked all the mountains in parts of southwestern Arizona on a regular basis. Steep hikes always killed me, thus, I was hoping that this wouldn't be steep. From what I read; it was a short hike down a steep hill but it didn't sound long. Then again, we will have everything we need on our backs, something to keep in mind.

I planned to keep my items to a minimum, taking into consideration that I never fared well with steep inclines or with anything on my back. However, pushing myself out of my comfort zone seemed to be consistently done. I wanted to conquer what was too hard.

Why did I continually take myself on steep hikes that were too hard? I could think of a dozen of them and I always needed help getting to the top or the end, or I struggled to do it myself. Something to contemplate. It seemed to be a need of mine to examine myself regularly to understand every nuance of myself. The way I studied myself was like the way we study the cosmos, the ocean, and the brain.

The detailed instructions for the quest listed what to bring and what to expect. Everyone signing up had to bring along all of their needs plus their food and drinks. Hawk provided the experience, wisdom, guidance, the knowledge of the quest site, and that was what I was looking for—a wise soul to help me figure out my roadblocks and help me find a path forward. Interested people were told to send a letter of intent to Hawk telling him why you wanted to do a quest so he could determine if this quest was right for you and if you were 'quest material.'

Then I began to go online to order the proper hiking shoes, small tent (light weight), a little cook stove, backpack, sleeping bag, cigars, and everything I saw in the list of necessary supplies, and made a list of what foods I wanted to take along, how to get to Lower Scorpion Campground where we would gather, and what city was nearby for me to stay at until I was ready to head down.

It's interesting to note that everyone else took tarps to sleep under and a tarp to sleep on. I was the only one who took a tent. I had already slept on the ground, on sandbars, without a tent for a week rafting through the Grand Canyon and knew how that felt. It was too hot for a tent because first of all, we were in Arizona but also as the sun set, the rocks and sand radiated the heat that was soaked up all day right back into the atmosphere. And everything that was out at night in the desert could crawl on me. I could feel things at night tickling my skin and chose to tough it out and work hard at sleeping through that mind game of wondering what that tickle was. I knew, from living in Arizona for years, off and on, too, what lived in the desert. I saw, first hand, all of it. So why did I have to have a tent? Because I knew what was out there but Hawk did too. He didn't have a tent. I also believed that I would sleep better knowing that nothing could crawl on me. All of this is a part of my shadow, I think. The shadow side of us is the part we don't want to look at, such as fears.

I got to Lower Scorpion Campground early, believing that it would be good for me to experience solo camping; it seemed wise and why not? What's the worst thing that could happen? I set up at a campsite near the road but just a bit back, under a small tree in the corner of one site by some interesting petroglyphs, and the bathroom was nearby.

A whiskey and coke cocktail and lit a cigar were my first initiation. It was time to sit awhile on a picnic table and think about what was unfolding. I looked at it like this: 'What am I putting myself through in order to continue to be a better person'? What do I hope to achieve by pushing myself out of my comfort zone?

That night I froze in my little one-man tent with, as it turns out, a summer sleeping bag. Number one lesson, why is my sleeping bag not sufficient? And every noise I heard creeped me out. Is it a person or an animal? Turns out I am not as brave as I think I am.

In the morning, sitting beside a fire, lost in my thoughts and savoring my coffee, a hiker limped into camp with anguish on her face. I was happy to see her walking in alone. One person I can get to know, a crowd not so much. She was loaded down with a huge backpack, one that is used for thru-hiking, and had a few piercings and tattoos on her face and arms, and had that telltale dusty look, shoes all worn and caked with dirt, legs very brown and weathered. First impression 'that girl is working on her baggage.' All the piercings and tattoos led me to that idea. She exchanged a few words with me then sat down to look at her foot. Her left foot was in extreme pain and she groaned as she unwrapped the 'ace' bandages from it. She said she did the entire thru-hike of the Appalachian Trail in six months when I asked her about that trail. It has always been a dream of mine to hike that. Automatically, she is my hero. Now she said she was hiking from Mexico to Canada, alone again. Such braveness always got my instant admiration and respect. She said her trail name was Threshold and she was on her own personal version of a vision quest. There is always more than one way to 'skin a goat,' as my mother used to say.

I was cooking my burger on the grill and offered to share with her.

She thanked me but said, "No thanks I'm vegetarian."

She added that she needed to get to the Visitor's Center, early the following morning and I heard her unspoken message. She was hurting and needed help getting there. I offered to make that happen when we both woke up.

I left her alone sensing that she needed her space and walked to a table, a little farther back in the park, and got lost in my own thoughts. I thought about the kinds of love I knew about: 'friendship love': I can walk away from that without sadness, at least the kinds I've known to this point; 'birth family love'—hurts, is destructive, lonely, empty, abusive, unavailable, and I feel better without the pain of it but at the same time I long for it; 'love from my kids and granddaughter'—I miss it a lot when I'm away from them, it fills me up, makes me feel valued and nurtured, I'm sad without it, and I'm lonely without it.

I did a mini vision quest before the real deal and it was fruitful. I needed to stay with the feelings that arose, the sadness, the heartache. Hiking around the area was a good way to familiarize myself with the land and to ponder what I had inside that needed to come out; being alone was key to letting that happen.

That night I slept in the back of my Toyota 4Runner hoping to get a better night's sleep and feel warmer, but I still froze. In the morning when I woke, Threshold was standing next to my car ready to roll. On the way to the Visitor's Center, I told her how I kept freezing at night and she told me, with the wisdom of a true hiker,

"Your bag is probably a summer one. Get the winter one rated for 15 – 20 degrees."

I cringed wondering, *why didn't I think of that!* I told her I was going on a vision quest and she said something that I thought about many times later.

"I hope you get what you *need.*"

What I 'need,' not what I 'want.' Interesting.

I drove back to Silver City, got the right bag and spent a couple nights in a motel to wait out the meet-up date. I knew a few things about myself already and the quest hadn't even begun.

A good way to bring about change, it turns out, is to go primitive camping. The day will start when you wake up, your sleep quality will depend on your environment, the temperatures, the quality of your sleeping bag, and on your fears. My nights were always interrupted by noises. I think I'm fearless but noises make me hyperalert wondering, what's out there? Fear still lives with me, it turns out. I thought of myself as fearless, previously.

Thoughts:

Severance: what parts of my life do I wish to bury, say good bye to, leave behind. What attitudes, stances, situations, habits, no longer serve me?

Answer: The person my family said I was. The person who was afraid of not being good enough, smart enough, pretty enough, interesting enough. The person who was afraid to speak her mind and stand up for herself. I want her gone.

Incorporation: what do I wish to call into my life, integrate, take on, accept? Are there aspects of a new life that call to me?

Answer: I wish to realize, celebrate and believe in my intelligence, inner beauty, wisdom, and the desire to always do the 'right thing.' I wish to honor my strengths and begin to protect myself from others who do not value, love, or appreciate me. I need to accept that just because I have a family, it doesn't mean there is love there. Aspects of a new life that call to me are the freedom to travel and fill my life with adventure, ways to help others who struggle, the ability to get my writing out there so that others can learn from my journey.

Threshold: what are the monsters in my life? What do I really fear? What blocks me from letting go of what I wish to sever from?

Answer: The monsters are my mother who seems to despise me, my father who seems to see me as attractive (dangerous), my sister who either resents me, is jealous of me or simply does not like me. I once feared never fitting in with my birth family. I fear abandonment, running out of money, not having a place to live, being unable to win love. I fear not learning to stop begging for love-performing for love. What blocks me is not knowing if I have a tribe to rely on, people who will have my back.

How to manifest: who are my allies, what are my sources of strength, what is my higher power, what tools do I have to call on?

Answer: My allies are few, they are my kids and two good girlfriends. My sources of strength are many, I am very loyal, very driven and disciplined, have high integrity, a mighty work ethic, a passion for learning, growing, adventure, connection, self-examination. My higher power is my soul and maybe nature; trees, hiking, streams, the sea, the wind, silence, meditation, reflection, self-love. The tools I have to call on are the very things I built in order to survive my childhood experiences. I am resilient, self-actualized, fiercely protective, self-sufficient, smart, wise, and a devoted 'listener.'

While I was hanging out in Silver City, enjoying the comforts of a motel room and restaurants, my old car's back window, which rolls down into the bottom of the door got stuck at an angle, and when I tried to force it, it wouldn't go anywhere. I decided to keep working it (this is something about me that is important to note—I do things until they work), I got that thing far enough down to lower the gate but when I did, it dropped and the window fell out onto the parking lot smashing into a gazillion pieces. That was unfortunate! And Embarrassing. I had to go into the office and ask for a broom and dust pan to sweep up all the glass. And the worst part was now I had no way to safeguard my stuff in the car. All I could do was take out the most valuable things and hope for the best. This definitely was one of those things that skews a person's plans. But there were no options. Now my warm camp in the back of the truck was wide open to whatever wanted to come in. That basically was the universe saying, "Get over it!"

I returned to camp and walked over to the petroglyphs. I stood by a humongous, smooth boulder to observe the etchings. The boulder looked like it had the markings of being used by the Native Americans because it looked like steps were chiseled into it. While I stood there, lost in the view, a lizard climbed on my arm. We both had a heart attack right then! I flicked him off and he was airborne.

I was celebrating my courage to do this quest thing. While I was preoccupied, a critter snatched my bag of chips, tore it open, and spilled it all over the ground. Next, a swarm of red ants jumped in to enjoy the treat. A few days ago, I was able to leave food out, but no longer. Nice warning, not that I have options. It's a free-for-all now.

Of course, it rained that night and blew right in on my feet. It made me laugh. I was getting tested before the damn quest even began. My grill and picnic table are now sitting in the middle of a pond.

The quest folks gathered and got set up at the next campsite, west of me, and walked over to say 'hello' and invite me to join them. Hawk, our guide; Kat, from Montana, and Meg and Charlie both from different parts of Wisconsin—my new team. Looking at them, there was no way to know how we would come to know each other, our weaknesses, our strengths, our beauty, and how we will help each other to overcome, see clearly, and work through whatever it is we need to learn here. We will become intimate with each other's struggles and pain and listen to understand how to help clarify what is showing up, and we will all cry in front of each other. It's just how things roll on a quest like this.

Hawk is passionate about what he does and he is a rock star at it. He knows things from years of study, experience, and trial and error, as well as his own deep suffering that helped him know what tools he needed, and strengths he had to help others heal. He, like everyone here and everyone everywhere, is never done doing the work and examining the path they are on. It is a very rich, valuable, gift we are blessed with when we do our own work. The epiphanies can set us on fire.

Hawk led us in talks about the Medicine Wheel and the four directions. South is us as babies, West is us as adolescents, North is us as adults, and East is us as elders. He smudged with sage over and around him, and passed it to each of us to sage ourselves and our surroundings, and asked us to say our 'gratitude prayer;' what we personally are grateful for. After he talked about each direction, he asked if it is why we are here. As babies, we are dependent; as adolescents, we begin our inner investigation; and as adults, we provide mature wisdom. As elders, we need to lean on others.

Like the four legs on a table which have to be equally balanced, we need to be adults but allow the innocence and trust of babies to live in us, to continue doing our inner investigation, and we need to lean on others now and then. We need a piece of all four directions.

The rain is ever-present but we just keep on keeping on. At one point, we spread a tarp over our heads to give us a reprieve from the cold and wet. Sparrow is oblivious to the weather. It seems to be a part of his focus to not let the weather interfere with what we are doing. It is cold and we are wet, but we proceed. We build a big bonfire to help warm us up. It's a real test for all four of us to keep our focus on what we're here for and 'not' on the rain, being cold, shivering, and wishing for warmth!

I began the sharing of 'why' I came here. I said I wanted to be like Michelangelo's David, chipping away all that is 'not' me to find what 'is' me. I want to uncover the core of who I am, shedding all that was written on my wall (all that I was told I am). Every one of them asked questions and then shared why they came. It was emotional for all of us to have four people completely take in what we are saying, really hear us, have constant eye contact, and interpret what we need from them in feedback to aid us on our journey. We all cried.

Ritual: Hawk told us that when we do our solo quest, which is four days of camping alone and fasting, we should look for a spot in the woods where the internal and external landscape say 'yes' to each other. Ask permission to stay there. Let yourself be led. The site should be a mirror of what you're searching for.

What I picked was a camp close by so I could conserve my energy for the hike out. It is obvious that I am already concerned about how I will handle that steep hike. My camp had a huge firepit and was right next to the river. The site was open and yet felt safe, people hiked by so not entirely private but overall a great spot for me. The fire aspect has always been important; every part of it, the cutting of the wood, the stacking of it, the burning, the smell, the warmth, and the sight.

Being near the river was also important. I am a water person and find it calming and meditational, the sounds and smell make me happy. I wasn't looking for privacy and was not afraid to camp here alone because my teammates and Hawk were in the vicinity. This site did mirror the basic ingredients for happiness, peace, and serenity for me. Wood supply, a fire, moving water, nature.

Fasting: what happens when you fast for those four days; it changes your consciousness. It's a sacrifice; an offering and it makes something sacred. The irony of fasting in the woods is that when there is no food, no cabinets, no refrigerator, no food smells, nothing to remind you of food, you actually do not suffer. You don't get weak or feel hungry. You are busy focusing on what you came here to do. And Hawk gave us plenty of tools to keep us focused.

Stone Pile: this is our one thread of connection to each other during the solo fast/camp. For me, it was Hawk who shared this. Every morning, early, he went to my pile and laid something there, a rock, a branch, a cairn, or anything to let me know he was aware of where I was and was checking on me. Each afternoon I visited the pile to lay something there to let him know I was okay. Meg, Kat and Charlie would do that for each other as well.

Since Hawk said that our culture is not designed to feed our soul, we have to feed it ourselves, find ways to nourish it. It is imperative that we do this because each one of us is vital to the well-being of all of us. On this quest, we helped each other understand what we needed to lead us to our true path and work through our old pain.

Death Lodge Ritual: it is a severance ritual of saying goodbye, to speak about anger, resentment, disappointment, and letting go. You make a circle with rocks, smudge the circle, walk into the center, sit there, feel the sun and the wind, meditate, and whoever enters your mind, enters the Death Lodge. Speak to them out loud. Pace yourself. Do it in stages. It doesn't have to be people alive today or it can be animals. When you have given it enough time, close the Death Lodge. Announce out loud that the Death Lodge is closed, say a prayer to the trees, rocks and dismantle the Death Lodge.

My former partner, Miles had died just before I went on the quest. He recently came back into my life to seek support while he went through some serious health issues. And I helped him through them. It was an opportunity to show up and give human kindness when needed. My father had died many years before and I needed to think about what he brought to my life, the good and the bad. My mother was still alive but was the most important person in my life, yet the most challenging and the most difficult to understand. My daughter, Jen, and teammate, Kat, showed up at the Death Lodge and I see them both as rescuers. I guess they were there to have my back.

Calling in the Dark Ritual: this is a way of facing or confronting our shadow to integrate them (parts of our lost selves, parts of ourselves we don't like or try to pretend are not there). This ritual must happen at night. Create a circle, be in it for the ritual. Call out "I'm ready, come and show yourself." Wait until you sense something. Then ask, "Who are you and what do you want from me?" The shadow side of us is very stealth at blocking our path and hiding from our conscious mind at the same time. What we fear, or don't like about ourselves we try to ignore but it never goes away unless dealt with, faced, and challenged. For me, it is the fear of not being accepted for who I am, recognized for being smart, and for being a solid, good human being.

Purpose Circle: this ritual is done the last night of the fast but I did it all four days. Build the medicine wheel with the four directions and smudge the area. Decide how long you want to sit there; it could be all night if you want. Sit in the middle of the medicine wheel, claim your purpose aloud, pray for a vision, meditate, feel your purpose becoming clear to you. When you feel complete, do the final smudge, close the circle, say a prayer of thanks, and dismantle the circle.

I started with South, the direction that stood for us as babies. I felt unloved and disliked by my mother and sister from as early as the age of two and a half. That phase of my life had to be examined. I had to understand why they saw me as a reject or a threat. I remembered that there were women who stepped up and 'took care' of me and I needed to think about how lucky I was that they saw my need. Two cousins, an aunt, and a neighbor, all took me under their wings and did what they could to give me attention. My baby self was left to grow up without love and nurturing, without being held, seen or heard.

The West, the direction representing adolescence, was a scary time for me. My father began to try to touch me inappropriately, and I had to be on guard at all times to protect myself because no one else was going to. My mother had shown that even though she was in the house, she never stepped up to put a stop to his behavior. It was on me to handle him. I was about 12 or 13. Though I craved love, I couldn't accept it from him, no hugs; no alone time. I couldn't take that chance. And I was attacked when I was about twelve, coming home from babysitting late at night. A man jumped out and forced me to the ground. I was able to get away but that event scarred me for years.

East represents a young adult and at that time, I was so far from realizing who I was and my value and power that I allowed mean and unkind behavior and treatment, and that went on for many, many years before I learned. I was continuing on with the treatment I got at home from my parents. I began my inner work after my kids left home, I was divorced, and ready to leave everything behind to be nomadic for many years. Much time was spent studying self-help books, spirituality, and adventure stories, to glean what I needed to learn.

The North phase, the crone stage that stood for wisdom as well as leaning on others for help, was where all the growth, self-love and acceptance was realized. All the study and work began to shape me into the person I wanted to be. Thus, most of my work was in the first three directions. That's where I had to examine, take apart, understand, and let go of the pain and sadness.

Severance Rituals: burning to rid yourself of things. Burying things that you want to die. Casting things to throw them away. Breaking things, ridding parts of us or our lives that don't work. Smashing, cutting, washing, mud bathing walking away from, retiring. All ways to sever what is not serving our higher selves.

I burned wood the entire time I was at camp. There were many parts of myself I wanted to get rid of. I hated feeling less than, hated feeling that I couldn't stand up for myself, protect myself, and express myself. It felt like I could not say what I wanted to say, ask for what I wanted and needed, and walk with pride in who I was without cowering, feeling like I still had to protect my heart and femininity from those I felt threatened by; my mother, father, and sister. I hated not being able to overcome what I saw as weakness. I hated falling back into that old behavior whenever I was around those three.

Ironically, to my surprise, I got cleansed while talking to 'Ponder Pine,' on the slope beside my firepit. Considering that I had no food in me, I was caught off-guard when suddenly I had explosive diarrhea. The only jeans I brought along, and my underwear now had to be removed, and a bath in the river as well as laundering those clothes was now my focus. My son sent me a smoking jacket and the smoking jacket would now serve as my skirt.

Incorporation: bringing things in, walking into, entering into, immersing oneself in, baptizing in. Make a circle, bring in energies of support you want to bring into your life. Pick up a rock, stick, or object in nature and put your intention into it and then drop it into the river.

I wanted to bring in love, acceptance, non-judgement, kindness, self-love, belief in myself, and clarity of purpose. I sat beside the river and spent considerable time on this ritual.

Take on: to wear, carry gifts from the earth: leaves, rocks, feathers, sticks, bones, and ask permission to take that thing and leave something in return like some of your hair.

I made a walking stick and carved things into it and added feathers. Those were my gifts from the earth. Carving prayers into a hiking stick or rings on it or around it felt right.

Other actions: cut your hair, change your style and look. Burn a log, as it burns and turns to light, put the energy into it that you want to get rid of. My brother used to say that trees soaked up sunlight all their lives and when they died, were cut down and burned, the glow of the fire was all that sunlight flowing back. One thing I found helpful was writing down on small slips of paper what I wanted to bring into my life as well as what I wanted to remove, and then one by one, burning those words, focusing on each one with intention, and feeling it happening.

Present your ego to a tree. Find a tree that speaks to you. Ask it what your schtick is. Tell it about your ego, in other words. Hawk says we all have one. For five minutes present your schtick to the tree, pause, ask the tree for its comments. I picked a tree on the slope near my camp. I called it Ponder Pine. I don't feel like I have much of an ego. Humility seems to be at my core. But that is probably my ego-self tricking me. If anything, my ego may be me trying to cover up for my insecurities.

Being in the moment rituals: use your senses to see the world or see it through our feelings, thinking and intuition/imagination. Anything we can do to use our senses, feelings, thinking, intuition, and imagination brings us more into the moment. Gaze at a tree close up, gaze at a river close up, lay on the ground and look up at the trees or sky; listen to the sounds around you, the birds, the wind in the trees; gaze at a fire, walk barefoot, wade in the river.

I had a great time doing this one. I studied the water in the river's edge, laid on the ground in the leaves, and studied the trees, leaves, branches, and the sky and clouds. I loved doing this. I could hear the birds chirping, the wind blowing through the trees, and the squirrels racing up and down the trees swishing their tails, playfully. Gazing at the fire is one of the most peaceful, meditative experiences for me. I can get lost in that act. It puts me into a trance that dissolves every ounce of tension inside myself. I waded in the river and crossed to the other side. Nature heals, for sure.

Rituals that bring out emotions—the truth mandala: make a circle, make two lines that divide it into four equal parts. Put something in each part. Mark 1 FEAR, mark 1 ANGER, mark 1 GRIEF/LOSS, mark 1 EMPTINESS. Step into one quadrant, speak everything you feel about that theme. Stay until it's done, until you work and express your truths about your emotional world. Close by standing in the center and saying, "Now I want to speak about HOPE." Proclaim there is hope in the world. In the EMPTINESS quadrant, I felt that emotion during my entire marriage. It was the loneliness time of my life. In the FEAR quadrant, I was afraid of being alone with my father, of walking alone at night after being jumped, and of never fitting in with my family. In the ANGER quadrant, I was very angry with my mother for setting me up to fail; she played the victim card, and I, seeing that, stood up to protect her, yet she didn't protect me. Finally, the GRIEF/LOSS quadrant. I mourned the brother who was the most loving, my brother Jack, who died when I was five and he was eleven. I mourned for my youngest brothers all becoming alcoholics, engineered by my father; and fearing they would not live long.

Imagination is power: Dreams activate imagination. Put intentions into having dreams. Keep a journal next to you at night. Ask for purpose before sleeping. Ask in an image-rich way. Ask a rock-picture, it is listening to you. Let the animal in the dream tell the story. Ask it to walk with you. I had a dream about my mother and in it, I saw that she was a woman without feeling, devoid of empathy, like an empty shell. I want to work on this area more and see if I can learn from my dreams.

The actual vision quest began at 10:30 in the morning of May 18, 2015. It was cold down there that spring! We followed Hawk, in our own vehicles, from the campsite to a parking area near a path that led straight down a steep descent. I already knew I was in deep shit just looking at it. We all hopped out of our cars and loaded up our backpacks with the help of each other. I was almost deep breathing just knowing what was ahead. I made sure there were only absolute essentials in my pack, nothing frivolous, but still felt serious concern about whether I could make it.

I am 71-years-old at this point. Hawk is probably in his sixties and Charlie is right up there with Hawk. The girls were in their twenties, I'd guess. Charlie had a ton of stuff he was carrying which, in metaphor speak, said that he needed a lot of stuff or had a lot of baggage. I took the lightest load, willing to go without rather than make my load heavy and yet my pack was crushing. Kat's pack was enormous and Meg's was just right. And she was fit like Hawk was.

In no time, with Hawk in the lead, hiking down at a fast pace, me following him and the girls after me, and Charlie in the back, I was struggling with the weight of my pack and the steep trail. My pack felt like it was going to force me to 'faceplant' because the trail was so steep, and I kept stopping. Kat stepped up and took my pack on top of her enormous backpack.

Anxious over being unfit for the hike, I struggled even without the pack. I think that even though I don't have anxiety issues, typically, I do have issues surrounding being left behind. That might be part of what I had to deal with on this trip.

Letting Kat help me and being vulnerable were two of my issues. Trusting someone to actually step up and help me was huge. I was used to hearing, "You'll live," from my mother. Letting Kat help me and feeling huge gratitude for it was quite a wakeup call. In essence, no matter what or where I was on this quest, my issues were smacking me in the face.

Hawk showed me three of his favorite campsites, once we were settled in base camp and everyone else took off to find their ideal spot. I told him I wanted to stay close to conserve energy for the return hike out on an empty stomach. I chose the first of his favorites. It was me. It had my favorite things, the river, and a firepit. There was a beach and a shallow spot to cross the river if I wanted to.

I put my tent up at base camp and sat waiting for Charlie and the girls to come back from their search. They took a long, long time and it wore Charlie out. They spent a lot of energy finding the perfect spot. Charlie came back exhausted. It was so clear that we were all showing who we were every step of the way in the choices we made, our actions, and what we took on this hike. And the two who were immediate responders to my needs were Kat and Charlie.

My former partner, Miles, was dying when I left for the quest and he died before it began. He will be a part of my Death Lodge. Meg said she felt he was with us on our hike down. That gave me insight into her. She was the one it took me the longest to know and understand but I liked that she was psychic.

The first day of the fast Hawk woke us up at the crack of dawn singing "Morning has Broken." We packed up and he had us form a circle around him so he could say a prayer over us, smudge us, and send us on our way with his blessings. Each prayer was personal to each one of us. One by one, we stood in front of him as he prayed over us, smudged us, and sent us on our way. Then we did a group hug and as each one's prayer was said, they walked off into the woods to head to their camp. I was touched by this ceremony. It felt loving, kind and personal.

I built cairns along the path from the 'stone pile' that Hawk designated as ours, to my camp to make sure I found it every day. I put together my camp, put the tent up near the edge of the slope that led to the river, hung my backpack on a tree branch, was happy to see the sun shining on the other side of the river, and started building a fire. It was a good way to make the place feel right for me.

Hunger comes and goes away instantly. I napped, off and on, beside the fire and then got busy gathering wood. Without tools I dragged entire branches that were three to four times the size of my firepit, up to ten feet long, back to camp knowing that I could just stick one end in but would have to stay close to make sure I didn't start a forest fire. Another thing to notice. I didn't have a choice in the wood I burned but I did keep myself close to the fire because of those extralong logs. I was responsible for protecting the environment while trying to find comfort in my primitive camping experience. Figuring out how to spend my time in this new setting was key to seeing who I am.

I went to the river thinking about the gifts I wanted to make for my team. It was the first thing I focused on. I picked a rock for Charlie. He had shared with us that his dad was his problem. His dad never approved of him, they never got along. The rock was my way of reminding him that 'his dad was not his rock to carry anymore.' I told him to throw that rock in the river and watch it go. For Kat, I wanted to have a star of some kind because she was a rock star for me.

I spent the day filtering water from the river, building a labyrinth, sunbathing, and then washed my jeans and underwear in the river, and laid them on a big rock to dry. I bathed in the river and it felt good to get clean. I don't watch TV so I don't miss that, but being alone with nature is something quite different to get comfortable with. For instance, okay, I can do whatever I want but what is there to do? Haul more wood, wade across the river, build a medicine wheel on the beach, be in the moment with my thoughts? Who I am was all right there to see. What would I do? How would I use my time?

I decided to do the Death Lodge. I put a big log in the fire and started with Miles because he has been on my mind a lot lately. It's hard to believe he's dead. He died a month after leaving the ranch. I spent four years with him, learned so much from him, and suffered so much with him, as well. He helped me understand that as I became enlightened, the length of my relationships with people would get shorter and shorter until I knew in a moment who was good for me and who was not; who was my tribe and who wasn't. I went from 28 years in my marriage to seven years with a farmer, to four years with Miles, and to one year with a guy who was the age of my oldest child. Now I think I have to have a relationship with me.

Next in the Death Lodge was my mother and then my three brothers, two of which were still alive at that time. I didn't choose my youngest brother, Todd, who died three years ago, for some reason. Kat popped in after Miles and then my daughter popped in. I said a prayer for Hawk who I see as a great example of a well-rounded person, someone I admire and aspire to learn from. My dad pops in. Then I drift off reflecting about where I want to live next.

Food crosses my mind now and then, and I imagine what I would cook for myself if I could. I walked to the beach and did the Sun Salutation and vowed to do that every day. I went to my tent around 5:00 because I was sleepy. I wanted to lay down and think about how my day unfolded. It was good and peaceful, and I did just fine. Tomorrow I will begin making the purpose circle. I am a planner and am doing it right here. It is who I am and also a list maker.

I slept 13 hours, I guess this experience is exhausting. I'm not hungry. Important to note and went straight to building a barn-burner fire and stared up at the mountains across the river. I saw rocks that looked like an Indian woman holding a child, sitting on a rock, looking adoringly at the mountain. I asked the mountain for my name. Hawk said that we should do this.

"Ask for your name," he said, "and you will get a spirit name."

I visited the stone pile and found that Hawk had left a little cairn on the rock and a circle of stones around the big rock. His kindness, caring heart, and gentleness are so obvious that it touches me. I add some rocks and a stick and head back to the beach to gather sticks for the gifts I want to make. I built a fire in the middle of my purpose circle and sat at the South rock to consider trust, innocence and childhood, and tried to envision what it is I need from this stage of life. In my childhood, there was no trust and my innocence was snuffed out early with no love or protection. The care was passive, mere essentials similar to how you would care for a dog. Food, water, clothes. A fire must be fed like a soul or heart for it to continue growing. It must be tended to, to keep it alive. What I needed, I continued to search for in my family and others, but maybe I needed to look inside myself to provide those things.

What I have been wanting from others, I must give myself to be a healer. I must heal myself in order to know how to heal others. A critter similar to a trilobite crawled over to me. They are extinct now but existed eons ago; maybe it is here to remind me that I am also an ancient soul or working from my ancient mind.

Thinking about trust and innocence; I want my mom to look at me, to hold me, to acknowledge me. She didn't and couldn't. I couldn't let my dad show me affection because he let me know very early on, when I was four or five, wh he was thinking about.

I decided to explore the other side of the river metaphor for exploring the other side of me. I have g great lengths to hide my light, my intelligence, my b my joy, and my soul with my mother, sister, and because these things threatened them, and my mother and sister retaliate when they see anything about me that is threatening. Jealousy is enormous. I decided it would be good to make a gift for me to represent the baby me who was not loved and nurtured, and keep her close to my heart.

I learned to speak minimally because people either cut me off, talked over me, or ignored me. I understand that my sister and mom saw me as a threat because my dad was attracted to me, and because I was born looking like my dad's mom. And then to top things off, my parents named me after my dad's girlfriend. You can't make stuff like this up. I was born blond and cute, and my mother and sister made sure I felt ugly, and I did my entire life.

Across the river, there was a shelf for me to sit on and I pondered the universe from there. I saw a school of minnows and they reminded me of my dad. When he took us fishing, he would net some minnows for our bait to use for catching perch and other small fish.

Poem I made for Kat:

This star gift is a metaphor for the star that you are. Your 't was dimmed once upon a time but no more! You have ht and energy of our sun, and I believe your destiny you and the world.

r Charlie:

is a metaphor for the rock you carry that is o longer need to carry him, throw this rock arry away your little boy's pain. You are a se time has come to honor the gift that

136

You are love, you are kindness, you are light. Watching you unfold your gifts before me/us, humbled me. You raised the bar in being human. I feel so lucky to have chosen to quest with you.

For Meg:

I made the Universal Om sign on a stick, the symbol of oneness. It took me longer to see Meg's inner beauty and heart but in time I saw that she also had a strong inner knowing, was very smart and very loving.

I came here wanting a vision for helping women but I realized now that I have to help myself first. I have my own work to do first. My daughters are quick to point out that I am a cheerleader for them but wonder if I do that for myself. I do, now. But I'm still a work in progress, an unfinished work of art.

Sitting by the river, I found an old oak tree and laid in the sticks, pinecones, and leaves beside it, and took a nap. Napping seems to be a go-to thing for me here. Inner work is apparently exhausting. And admittedly, there is an underlying fear of wearing myself out with no food for fuel.

Later, sitting with socks on my feet, soaking them in the water, the water looked lifeless. But that was an illusion. With a closer look, I saw little gold things that looked like sediment darting around with no logical direction. Teeny fish like minnows swarmed and two tadpoles joined th fray. No one was prey or a threat, they all just did their thi in harmony in a small puddle of water.

I am feeling sleepy again, it is late afternoon. Tomo I will make the gifts for my team, do yoga, walk acr river to my meditation shelf, do the stone pile, an purpose circle, this time doing East.

If my campsite mirrors me, it mirrors what I am searching for. The fire warms me and gives me reflection. The river gives me peace and reflection, and I can learn from it. I like how it never forgets to flow, how it stays fresh by flowing steadily, and how it cleanses itself by continuing to flow. I like the fire because it lights up the dark, it adds warmth to the day and to me, the flames dance, and the fire willingly ignites me using what is abundant here, dry leaves, needles, pinecones, dead branches, and juniper needles.

Fasting: it is a sacrifice, an offering, makes my quest sacred. It has been easy. Hunger visits briefly and passes just as quickly. I am so happy for that!

Time to do the Death Lodge, speak about anger, resentment, disappointment, letting go.

In a moment of introspection, I thought about how I always wanted to be good, nice, low maintenance, easy, so I caused no trouble. The 'nice girl.' Now I want those behaviors to die. I want to be the opposite, swing the pendulum far in the other direction.

My body is getting a rest with no food intake, thus no
sing. After 71 years, my body gets a full four-day rest.
mmingbird visited me three nights at my tent. They
l of tenacity and endurance in the pursuit of our
gh they are tiny, they are very sociable and
oping in close to human beings. They are
and bringers of love, good luck, and joy.
to bring love to the person who spots

e
ng
rrow
ss the
do my

my breathing is associated with
, fear, and having the air knocked out
mother. Now I know where to focus.

138

That idea was so deeply buried. The mountain gave me a spirit name. It is 'freedom.' And nothing means more to me than being free.

I think when I got emptied out, sitting next to Ponder Pine, I also got emptied of thoughts but crammed a few more delightful things into this day; a bloody nose and a dream. I dreamt a man fell on his face on the steps in front of me. I asked the little boy with him what he did just before falling. He said he ate so I gave the man the Heimlich Maneuver. Dreaming about cleansing!!!

Hawk left his signature gift at the stone pile, four rocks, four different colors, in the four directions.

The river is doing what it does best. I must do what I do best: listen, observe, hear people, and care.

I'm thinking about food more. I am beginning to feel anxious about getting out of the canyon with my backpack on with an empty stomach. Hiking up is harder. My thoughts on that, get to the top

- of the trail,
- of the canyon,
- of my mission,
- of my business/career.

In order to see the sacred in all the things, I have to se it in me. I have to see my preciousness, my brilliance, a my wisdom.

A bee, a daddy long legs and a trilobite all came t I must look like a part of nature now. Maybe I even like nature.

All I want to do is rest and nap today. Next to the fire, in the tall grass, I fell asleep again.

It is my last day. I have everything packed and ready. My hair is a rat's nest. I am mentally listing the foods I will eat when we get to the top. Little did I know that when we all gathered at base camp the next morning and Hawk had fresh fruit cut up for us with walnuts and oatmeal, it would gag me. I thought I would want to eat but food didn't feel good in my stomach.

I had a dream my last night at solo camp. My mom and I were standing in the driveway between our old house and the neighbors. I turned around and she was gone so I went into the neighbors and she was coming out of the bathroom. I said it felt weird there, sparsely furnished and she said, as she took my hand and looked into my eyes,

"I'll just start over, nothing stays the same, everything changes."

What does that mean to me? Meg said my mother lived life on her terms and was there but wasn't there.

At base camp, Hawk had us gather in a circle in the ⁿw and think about what we left behind, and what we ʰ us. We hugged and began our hike out. The girls ⁿd then me and Charlie followed. He said that ᶜollow me to make sure I came out. He didn't herwise. That's interesting. Hawk followed re that everything was back to normal at

lawk took Charlie's pack and Kat took ᵉver to get to the top but Charlie stayed e girls and Hawk waited for us at the ρ faster so I didn't hold everyone up but could not do it. At the top, Charlie had a cooler of beer and he gave us each a bottle and chips. What a treasure he was and that beer and chips was a godsend. We parted ways and headed for the little store. Showers were on everyone's mind along with food.

As we shared our stories with each other later, at camp, I learned that each one of us had family issues to heal and work through. When we sat in circle to hear what we each got, saw, felt, and learned on our solo fasting, as one spoke the others tuned in to soak up what was being said and how they interpreted it. They asked questions and then wrote in that person's journal. They gave their all, in understanding and giving feedback. It was emotional because none of us was used to being heard or cared about. Four people tuning fully into you and your story, your pain, thoughts, feelings, visions, and all that your quest taught you is emotional. Finally, you are getting something you have craved. It is a glorious feeling and yet a bit uncomfortable. How to handle all those emotions that want to flow out all at once? In that short time, complete strangers knew each other intimately and cared deeply about each other's well-being.

They all, in one way or another, reminded me that:

- I found community in the mountain and our group
- I needed to find the sacred in myself;
- was I running toward or away from things?
- I have a great ability to praise and honor others, can I do that for myself?
- The quest changed for me on the way downhill
- I carried weight but needed to accept gentleness and help

- I needed a sweet healing path rather than gutting it out
- I needed to nurture my masculine and feminine sides
- I needed to experience gifts internally before giving them to others
- I needed to 'stay home' in one place and look for internal and external 'home'
- Can I stay in one place if it has everything I need?
- Can I create something that I couldn't leave or don't want to leave?
- I run versus commit and am searching for commitment that I can trust
- My mom, in my dream, met on her terms, was there but not really
- I had quiet courage
- I was hiding myself from my family and was not able to explain myself in order to be understood

I took a white shirt of mine and wrote on the front of it what I wanted to move into. On the back, I wrote what I wanted to leave behind. In parting, Hawk warned us to be careful how much of our experience we shared with others and to be careful who we did decide to trust with our experience because if they didn't understand or support it, they might negate our experience. That we needed plenty of time to soak up all that we learned from our quest.

When we left and went our separate ways, I felt very good about it all and kept in touch with everyone for a long time until others drifted away into other things. Hawk set up a place for us to do that. I am so grateful that I took that chance to explore myself in this very unique way.

My Mom Befriended the Judge to Get My Ticket Waived

My mother, brother Peyton, and I were doing one of our many cross-country road trips from Arizona to Wisconsin with plans to do the return trip in two months, when summer was over. My brother, by then a serious alcoholic, always wanted to follow, convoy style, in order to bring all his tools along in his own car and spending ten hours or more without a drink nearly killed him. I was always cognizant of his needs and how he could suddenly crash and burn if I didn't pay attention to when he was hitting the wall. So, I cut the day short, and rolled into a motel in Clovis, New Mexico. We could check in, get some much-needed cocktails in hand and a nice dinner. Then all would be well.

After doing one complete circle of the property, I concluded that there was no way to park close to the entrance. My mother was old and needed every consideration. In her nineties, she was hunched over, her knees killed her, and she used a cane to get around. I looked at the one available handicapped parking spot and said to myself, *in this little podunk town no cops will be rolling through so no worry about getting a ticket*. I parked, grabbed our bags, helped mom into the lobby, and forgot all about it.

The following morning as we climbed into my car, there stuck to the middle of the windshield was a ticket! Mom went postal over it. She read it and began seething. She felt that this was hugely unfair. For the next few days on the road, she redundantly raged over the ticket and what she was going to do to correct it. It was hard to hear her constantly rage about it but I let her and hoped it would blow over. It didn't though.

When I dropped her and Peyton off in Lake Geneva, I forgot all about it but she didn't. She wrote the judge a letter. She wrote about how old she is and appealed to the judge's leniency. I didn't see her much over that time period so I literally forgot it. When I picked mom and Peyton back up to do our return trip, two months later, mom let me know she heard back from the judge. That lady not only agreed to tear up the ticket but she asked us to meet her for lunch, on her, at a restaurant she chose, on our return trip through Clovis.

I decided I had to make that happen because mom had gone to great effort to create that friendship, and I wanted to see her get rewarded for it, and I wanted her to feel like a winner. I texted the judge and set up a time and day to meet, and we headed West. On our second day, we showed up an hour early because I forgot the time difference but the judge quickly made it work for her. She walked in and I watched her, how she carried herself, her soft, kind, pretty face and her confidence.

She went over to Peyton first, shined her light on him, and poured love and respect into him. That in itself warmed my heart. Then she said, 'Hi' to me and moved over to sit in front of mom, and poured so much love and adoration into mom; it filled my heart with love for her. Mom glowed in her light and her love. It was a moment that was charmed and a moment I will cherish forever. She sat face to face with mom soaking her up like she was her own mom. I felt grateful that I knew how to make this moment come to fruition. It was pure gold.

The judge made me aware that she was here with us as long as we wanted to be here. She paid for our meal and when we parted ways, I knew that this whole trip was all about my mom and Peyton getting loved, respected, and valued.

It proved, once more, to me that there was no way to know how a plan would unfold. I could think I was the driver of the bus but, always, without exception, things played out far more interesting and surprising than I thought they would.

Todd had a saying, "Get out of your own way and let life happen."

This was one excellent example of that truth.